INTRODUCTION TO RAISED BED GARDENING

THE ULTIMATE BEGINNER'S GUIDE TO STARTING A RAISED BED GARDEN AND SUSTAINING ORGANIC VEGGIES AND PLANTS

PETER SHEPPERD

For Carmen; for being herself.

This checklist includes:

- 10 items you will need to kick off your green fingered adventure.
- The highest quality Gardening items.
- Where you can buy these items for the lowest price.

The last thing we want is for your gardening project start to be delayed because you weren't prepared.

To receive your essential tool checklist, visit the link:

www.petershepperd.com/gardening-checklist

CONTENTS

INTRODUCTION

'I grow plants for many reasons: to please my eye or please my soul, to challenge the elements or challenge my patience, for novelty or for nostalgia but mostly for the joy of seeing them grow.'

— DAVID HOBSON

A little over a decade ago, I bit into a tomato that I had just purchased from my local supermarket. It was perfectly formed, without bruise or blemish - it was also without taste. It looked totally different to those gnarled tomatoes that my grandmother used to grow in such abundance in her back garden, and which provided such mouth watering memories.

Figure 1. Freshly picked homegrown vegetables will fill your heart with pride.

That perfect looking, store bought tomato awakened a memory that set me on a journey - a quest to reproduce some of the delights that my grandmother grew with such nonchalant ease. She was extremely proud of her vegetable garden and it was always filled with a seemingly endless variety of edible wonders.

I wanted to reproduce that garden and all the adventures that went into creating it. The trouble was, I had no idea where to begin. The large scale migration to cities and the transformation of our society that we have witnessed in the last few decades has seen a rapid demise in the gentle art of gardening. Today we pick up nearly all of what we eat on a quick trip to the local supermarket or greengrocer. Somewhere along the way, the very natural process of growing our own foods was transformed into a mystery – a dark art that many seem to believe is beyond the reach of all but trained specialists.

The objective of this book is to guide the reader on a journey similar to the one that I have been on for so many years now. Along the way I hope to show that gardening is neither difficult nor complicated. My grandmother had no horticultural training and was still growing much of her own food until she was well into her eighties. Using her notes and the additional information I have gathered over the years, I have put together this book to show just how easy gardening can be.

My desire is that this series of publications will do more than just teach you how to grow your own healthy and nutritious vegetables. I hope that, as in my case, you will become more concerned about what you eat and the processes that go into producing that food. As farming has become more industrialised, and as we have placed more and more responsibility for our food production into the hands of large corporations, the food that we put into our bodies, and the bodies of our children, has changed. Vegetables are now chosen for their shelf life and their visual appearance rather than for the nutrition they offer or the taste they provide. Much of what we eat will have travelled thousands of miles before it reaches our plates and all the way along that journey it is shedding its level of nutrition.

If nutrition levels and flavour were the only losses in these giant production processes, then it might be a price we are prepared to pay in exchange for the convenience offered. Unfortunately that is not the case. To a large extent, it is the environment that carries the burden of our desire for convenience. Don't think that the perfectly formed tomato that travelled several hundred miles to reach you is the result of careful plant husbandry and exposure to the best that Mother Nature has to offer. It will almost definitely have been grown in a greenhouse using an obscene amount of chemicals and unsustainable quantities of water. Those poor souls that picked and packed it for you will probably have been paid a subsistence wage, whilst working on tenuous contracts – all this so that you can have gorgeous looking produce at a low price, whilst making fortunes for large conglomerates.

I believe that growing your own food is so much more than just a matter of putting food on the table and saving yourself a few pennies. It is a passion, an art, an exercise and an act of rebellion against a system that does not have our best interests at heart.

You can join that rebellion. This series of books will guide you through the growing process from start to finish. As one book builds upon the information that you gained in another, you will, almost by accident, find yourself developing a broad-based horticultural knowledge. You will learn the tools you need as well as those that are just nice to have. You will follow the growing process from soil preparation, right through to harvest, with a little bit on storage and preservation thrown in for good measure.

Above all, you will learn that gardening is not a lost art that disappeared along with our great grandparents. It is really very easy and requires little more than some basic techniques and a smidgen of enthusiasm. (If the enthusiasm is lacking don't worry – it will soon grow).

I have learned many things in the course of my own journey. Much of what I discovered really surprised me. I didn't know, for example, how much pleasure could be gained from sprinkling a few seeds onto

Figure 2. Passing on gardening wisdom.

some damp compost in an old ice cream tub. The

appearance of those first tiny leaves felt almost miraculous. Sitting down to a meal where every vegetable on the table was the result of my own labours was more rewarding than any three-star Michelin banquet.

There is something almost cathartic about plunging your hands into deliciously rich soil. Perhaps this is because, in doing so, we are returning to something that humankind has been doing for millennia. Something we were meant to do. We are retracing our roots back to their origins; back to a time before we got lost in the constant pursuit for more that seems to have gained such a grip on modern society. On this journey you will make many discoveries. You will learn that growing your own plants won't make you rich in ways that are now regarded as so important today. Instead you will discover an altogether new value system. Healthy food, exercise and the chance to engage in an activity that can be enjoyed by the whole family are things that are difficult to put a price on. I will leave it to you to judge their worth.

You will also learn that time has a different scale when gardening. Our lives seem to have become so rushed that merely slowing down has become almost impossible. Start gardening and you will learn that it is nature that dictates the pace and that hers is altogether different from your own. She won't be hurried, prodded or bribed.

Figure 3. Get your hands dirty.

This book is just one of a series of books that takes you across a whole spectrum of what is a very wide ranging subject. Most will start with an introduction to a specific subject so that you can get started as quickly as possible. There is nothing that kills desire more quickly than an overload of theory. After that there is a more advanced follow up that will take your knowledge to a higher level. I have deliberately avoided any subscribed order in which the series should be followed. Gardening should be fun and you are free to pick up those books on subjects that most please and motivate you. In writing these books, I did not set out to produce a dry theoretical masterpiece. Instead, I prefer to allow the reader to amble along the pathways of my own experience, making whatever detours and diversions he or she chooses to take along the way. As you are about to discover, this is a vast subject with many different ways of doing things. These books offer one route, but soon you will be experimenting and building ideas of your own, stealing methods from other gardeners and high jacking procedures from nature. That non-prescriptive way of learning is, in my opinion, what makes gardening such an interesting experience.

Figure 4. Harvested vegetables from your own back yard.

Finally, it would be unfair of me not to offer a word of caution from my own experience. Gardening is as addictive as nicotine or sugar, though without the health risks or weight gain. Dip just a toe into the water and the next thing you know you will be peering into neighbours' gardens, begging seeds and cuttings from total strangers and seeing allotments as educational opportunities. Previously nondescript window sills will metamorphose into greenhouses and you will begin to salivate at the sight of a tidy shed. Your dress sense will go all up the creek, or disappear altogether, and you will gather a collection of likeminded friends, the likes of whom you would never have met at that trendy wine bar on a Friday night. You have been warned.

1

WHY THE RAISED BED SYSTEM?

Humankind first started growing food deliberately in around 11000BC. This is believed to have taken place on what is known as the Fertile Crescent that runs from the northern lip of the Red Sea to the Persian Gulf. Prior to that, our ancestors had been simple hunter gatherers, following herds or picking edible crops as and when they ripened. When the first crop cultivation started, it was an adaption that would change the face of history forever. Once we could control the process by which food was acquired and grow it, it enabled us to settle in one place. This would have profound ramifications on human society that are still being felt today.

As our ancestors began staying in one place for more extended periods, we could no longer rely on simple temporary shelters and fixed structures began to develop. By 9000 BC, we had begun learning to store grain and with this, food security increased. Though it took more effort to grow food than it did to harvest it from the wild, it meant that man could gather ten to one hundred times as many calories per acre as he had been able to in the past.

Suddenly people were producing more food in a day than they could actually eat in that time frame and they could keep it for leaner periods. Shortly after that, some people were able to step away from the food production process and develop other skills such as metal or woodwork. This then led to the barter system where some people were able to survive without being involved in the food production process at all. These might not seem like dramatic changes, but they would have a significant impact on the future.

On the Fertile Crescent, it was possible to grow food because the seasonal rains were so reliable. Soon, however, people further afield would begin using primitive but effective irrigation systems and food production became more widespread and moved to other areas.

All sounds good so far. No need to go racing after potentially nasty wild animals with a sharpened stick or be dependent on beating the birds to that wild fig tree you found last year. Just throw a few seeds onto the ground and pretty soon you could put your feet up and wait for your freshly baked bread rolls to be delivered.

Why then has one scientist described the introduction of agriculture as the 'worst thing in the history of the human race?'

The answer to that is that the arrival of managed cultivation opened the door for large scale agriculture, all be it, many thousands of years later. That has brought with it massive problems. Industrial food production incorporated the widespread use of harmful chemicals for both pest control and weed elimination. If you are going to squeeze every cent you can out of a production system, then all competition has to be seen as the enemy.

Whilst those developments were almost inevitable when producing food on the scale that we do today, we are starting to pay the price for our conversion from hunter gatherer to industrialized consumers. Mega food industries will tell you that the use of these chemicals and synthetic fertilizers is unavoidable if we are to continue to feed our burgeoning population. Many will dispute that argument, but trying to change the entire world economic system is probably a little outside the scope of this book. Instead, this first in a series of books sets out to offer an easy to master and inexpensive way to produce much of your own food yourself. In doing that you will at least be able to control the produce you put into your body and what goes into that produce. A large part of the process will fall back under your management, and you will be able to decide how free it should be of synthetic additives and pesticides.

The book does not propose to make you totally self sufficient, but it will guide you to a position where you can grow many of the vegetable crops that you and your family eat. If you do choose to extend what you learn in these pages to producing all of your own fresh produce - that is certainly not beyond the realms of possibility and hundreds of thousands of people around the world do exactly that.

Once you take over the growing of your own vegetables, you are assured that they are free from harmful chemicals and that they have not travelled many thousands of miles to reach your plate. Not only will you be reducing the size of your family's carbon footprint and eliminating exposure to toxic products, but you will also notice a very different taste from those store bought vegetables. Your own produce will be higher in vitamins and nutrients and have a far smaller adverse impact on the environment.

Raised bed gardening has become a very popular option for the home grower and there are many practical reasons for this which we will look at shortly. Over the years, people have moved away from gardening due to the changes that have taken place in society and the way in which we now lead our lives. As a consequence of this, people have lost a valuable skill and over time, what was once a normal day to day activity has begun to seem like something of a mystery. This book sets out primarily to show just how straightforward gardening can be, and the raised bed system will really add to that simplicity.

Figure 5. There are many benefits of being involved in a community garden.

THE BENEFITS OF RAISED BED GARDENING:

- The first obvious benefit of raised bed gardening is the reduced physical effort placed on the gardener. Even if a bed is only nine or ten inches high, it means that the gardener doesn't need to bend so far and he or she can work the bed quite easily from a standing position or their knees if they choose to do so. Of course, the bed can be built higher and then even kneeling is not necessary. Gardening is, by nature, a physical occupation, but almost all of the aches and pain incurred are through bending rather than as a result of the digging or planting process. That is not to suggest that gardening has or will become a sedentary activity. It merely means that it now requires effort that falls into the comfortable and sustainable exercise category rather than the extreme sports arena.

I like to build my beds to two feet as that is a comfortable height for me to work at, while at the same time giving me plenty of depth in which to lay in the growing medium for my plants.

For the disabled, raised beds can really be a game changer. From being an inaccessible past time, raised beds suddenly bring gardening back into the realms of possibility for those in wheelchairs or with bending difficulties. For people deprived of so many of the activities that most of us take for granted, this can really open a whole new window of opportunity.

Figure 6. Different varieties of lettuce can be grown easily in a small space.

- As a first time gardener, raised beds offer an easier system to manage. Much of the preliminary digging that takes place at the start of each season is eliminated. At the same time, many of the weeds that would typically be encountered are destroyed because you are not planting directly into the ground. They are not designed to make their way through such a depth of soil. That doesn't mean that you will never be troubled by weeds. That is one curse that the gardener will always have to bear. However, those that do manage to self seed are easily picked out as they won't have deeply established root systems. What's more, you can reach them easily and will not have to resort to crawling around on your hands and knees looking like and obsessive yoga guru.

- When you plant directly into the ground you must first either till the soil or you must deep mulch it and wait many months for that mulch to break down before you can plant. With this system, once the beds are prepared they are ready to plant and there is no tilling involved. Every year the gardener simply adds more compost and soil ameliorants, digs it over lightly and the bed is ready for replanting.

In recent years there has been much study into tilling soil and there is a growing movement that advocates not doing so at all. When we till soil we break down its natural structure which makes it prone to both wind and water erosion. Each year we lose 24 billion tonnes of fertile soil to erosion. That works out to a staggering 3.4 tonnes of our most important non renewable resource per person. While doing this, we release tonnes of carbon dioxide into the atmosphere and kill many of the beneficial micro organisms that the soil contains. Just one teaspoon full of healthy soil contains more micro organisms than there are people on the planet.

- This system offers another advantage over growing plants directly into open ground. Crop rotation is critical when planting into the ground. Each crop will reduce that soil of the nutrients that it most requires. Over time a patch of soil can become so denuded that it can no longer support plants of certain kinds. On a large scale, vast quantities of fertilizer are used to replace this nutrient loss. Run off from excess chemical fertilizers is now a problem in many of the world's waterways and oceans. It also speeds weed growth thus leading to the use of excess herbicides. The commercial farmer can grow the same crop year after year in the same patch of ground because he is prepared to use synthetic fertilizer for all his plant nutrition.

To avoid this, crop rotation must be practised. In raised beds the soil is continually being topped up and having those nutrients replaced by good natural soil conditioners. Crop rotation simply ceases to be an issue. If you want to, you can plant the same crop in the same place for many years because, in effect, each time you plant you will be planting into new soil. This constant revitalizing of the growing medium is a crucial benefit in terms of raised beds and should not be underestimated.

As you delve deeper into this series, you will see that soil and its well being are crucial parts of the gardening process. Good soil is a valuable asset and, in short, if you don't have healthy soil, you won't grow healthy plants. That is, of course, unless you are simply prepared to replace the natural health of your soil with a vast cocktail of chemical ingredients. Unfortunately, most of the agro industry has now simply resigned to the fact that it will always use fertilizers to produce crops. The link between large scale farming and the chemical industries is now so entwined that it is difficult to see a way to separate them.

- Another advantage of raised beds is that pest control becomes a great deal easier. Flying pests will still need to be dealt with but other pests are far easier to manage. If you have ever gardened in an area where there are moles present then you will know what a nightmare they can be. They seem to have this incredible knack of snacking on the base of your root vegetables precisely one day before you had planned to harvest. When you arrive in the morning with your hopes high and a basket just begging to be filled, you suddenly discover that the carrots you had been nurturing for weeks are simply a pile of sad and withered leaves. If you do have moles then all you will need to do is lay a sheet of fine chicken mesh at the bottom of the bed before filling it and they won't get so much as a nibble from your crop.

Rabbits or deer may be a problem but the raised beds offer you something onto which you can easily attach netting to keep them out. The pests that most frustrate gardeners are slugs and snails. These ninjas of the night use an array of stealth tactics and an ability to stay up long after the weary gardener has gone to bed, to attack leafy crops. With a raised bed, sliding up the sides is already a deterrent, but you can increase the degree of difficulty by attaching a band of coarse shade cloth to make your bed into a natural fortress.

Flying insects are always going to find this system less of a deterrent than land bound critters. They will need to be subjected to all of the environmentally friendly pest control methods that you would use elsewhere in the garden and which we will look at in greater detail later in this series. The gardener's first defence against all pests, however, is his power of observation. An experienced gardener will know what signs to look out for, what plants are most vulnerable to attack and where about on the plant to find those signs. Raised beds are no substitute for experience, but they do at least bring the crops closer to the eye line. As with the deer and rabbit protection, raised beds are very easy to cover with hooped tunnels or shade netting and both of these options will help to protect against flying pests.

- The raised sides of a bed are exposed to the sun as opposed to planting into the grounds where the soil is cool. This can dramatically increase the growing season for your crops and that in turn will increase yields. Not only does the soil in your beds heat up earlier, but it also stays warm later. This allows you to get plants into the ground before you would if you were using conventional techniques, and then to keep growing longer.

Figure 7. Strawberry patch covered with mesh to protect it from birds and squirrels.

- If you are blessed with perfect gardening soil then drainage may not be an issue. (I have never met a gardener with perfect soil). Most people, however, need to really take drainage into consideration with traditional measures. It is something that is so often overlooked but which can lead to huge disappointment. Clay or a shallow sub soil layer can cause water logging and this really complicates the gardening process. Firstly it has to be dealt with which can delay the planting season. Secondly it takes longer to warm up and thirdly the clays tend to make the soil really difficult to work and far more physically demanding. If you have ever spoken to a gardener who has to work a heavy clay soil, you are likely to have heard him lament the problems that he has to overcome. He is always having to add sand and grit and each year he knows that the start of the season is going to be a difficult physical slog. What's more, if the weather suddenly goes dry, the clay can harden to a rock like consistency that plants struggle to deal with - with the exception of weeds of course.

In raised beds this is simply not an issue. You control the drainage by filling the bed correctly which you will soon see is very simple. After that drainage just isn't a problem and you can get straight down to planting your crops. You are no longer at the mercy of whatever type of soil it was that you happened to inherit. You are now master of the beds and in this godlike role you manage and you make up the soil so that it is in optimum condition at all times. This works for the gardener and it certainly works for the plants.

Even if you have the opposite problem and you are gardening on loose sandy soil where overly fast drainage is an issue, you can overcome it with this method. Though you control the planting medium in the actual beds, the soil beneath that may be fast draining. That problem can be overcome by applying a porous plastic membrane before you fill the bed. That will not stop drainage but it will slow it and in that way the problem is overcome. At the same time, the humus, compost and soil mix that you put into the bed holds moisture so you are assured of damp conditions that do not become overly waterlogged.

- Raised beds allow you to be far more targeted when it comes to watering. Traditionally it is just accepted that some water will be lost along paths which can also lead to erosion. As access is often tricky in normal beds, water is often sprayed quite long distances to reach the plants and this means that it does not always go where the gardener wants it to. Raised beds enable the gardener to water exactly where he wants the water to go and well managed soils hold moisture far better than lots of ground planted beds do. Water is becoming a precious resource and one that needs more consideration by all but especially the gardener who wants to work in collaboration with nature rather than against it.

- One of my favourite advantages of the raised bed system is that it enables the gardener to plant his crops far more densely than he otherwise might have. Because conditions are ideal, the gardener can plant many of his chosen vegetables more closely than he would if he were growing them in traditional rows in the ground. For one thing, he no longer needs to lose ground to footpaths running through the beds. With the raised bed method, and providing the beds have been built to the right size, the gardener has access from all sides of his bed and there are none of those narrow little paths creeping between the plants.

One of the options we will look at further into the book is to use what is called the square foot gardening method. This is a technique that was invented by an engineer called Mel Bartholomew many years ago and it simplifies the gardening process by breaking the bed into smaller more manageable chunks. You deal with one square at a time and research done over the years allows you to know precisely how many of each crop you can cram into each tiny square. This method dramatically eliminates inefficiency. For the inexperienced gardener it makes the whole process much less daunting as they are faced with just a small patch rather than a vast expanse. It becomes a simple case of breaking a large problem down into smaller and more manageable chunks. At the same time it leads to higher yields.

Figure 8. Raised beds are a wonderful way to connect children with nature.

I hope that this overview of the raised bed system has at least allayed any fears you might have about growing your own produce. The whole purpose of the raised bed system is to make the gardeners life easier and it certainly does that effectively. Simply by choosing this method, you increase yields and reduce potential problems in one foul swoop.

If some of the back ache is taken out of the process then gardening becomes so much more of a pleasure and that is the way that it should be. For many people living in cities, contact with nature consists of an occasional walk in the park, at most. This method really can change that because there are few areas where you come into deeper contact with nature than you do with gardening. Suddenly you find yourself relating to nature at a whole different level than you do as a pure observer sitting on a park bench. You are now intimately involved in the whole process from preparing the environment for the plant through to germination, growth and harvest.

Your appreciation of soil is about to change dramatically. You will cease to see it just as brown dirt and will start to recognize it as the living, giving raw material that it really is. As you reconnect with nature in a way that you never have in the past, you will start to have a whole different appreciation of the food that you eat and what goes into producing it.

The beauty of this system is that you don't need acres of land. In South Africa there is a charity that works in impoverished townships. They teach a similar method and show people how they can grow enough food to supply the vegetable needs for a family of four from a bed the size of a front door.

As an education source for small children there can be few activities that a family can engage in together that will produce more significant rewards. That connection with nature is something that small kids love and everything from handling their first earth worm to seeing their first seeds sprout will be a new adventure for them. Add to that the delight of being able to eat something that they have played a part in producing, and you soon overcome that all too common distaste for vegetables. Serve a kid a store bought carrot that he had no part in producing and you will often face rejection of the vegetable. If they have helped plant the seed and do the watering and harvesting themselves, then parents are far less likely to encounter this problem. Theirs is the generation that is going to bear most of the brunt of what the agro chemical industry is doing to this planet and this type of education will be their greatest defence.

I recognize that I have tackled this subject purely from the vegetable production aspect. That is what raised beds are most commonly used for, but there is no reason that this system should not be used for growing ornamental plants just as effectively. I have always felt that the vegetable patch is an overlooked area when it comes to visual impact but it is entirely possible to use ornamental garden design principals when setting up your garden. Later in this series we will look at some of the design principles you can use that can make your vegetable patch as attractive as any ornamental garden. By combining beautiful flowering plants into your planting scheme, you can add aesthetic appeal and attract useful pollinating insects at the same time.

I am a firm believer that the age of the scruffy veg patch, tucked somewhere out of sight, is over. We should all be considering combining beauty and functionality and cease to see edible plants as being unsightly. A well laid out and flourishing vegetable garden is a sight to behold and that beauty is augmented when combined with other non-edible plants.

Figure 9. Children can learn new skills and develop self-confidence by spending time in the garden tending plants and growing their own food.

REASONS TO USE RAISED BEDS - RECAP:

- Less physical effort required
- Far easier to manage
- Greater control of growing medium
- No need for crop rotation
- Better pest control
- Greater heat retention
- Eliminates drainage issues
- Improved water management
- Denser planting affords greater yields

2

BEFORE STARTING

"Tools of many kinds and well chosen, are one of the joys of a garden".
-Liberty Hyde Bailey

Raised beds are not a new invention. The pre-Hispanic people were using them as far back as 300 BC. Called Waru Waru, these beds were used because they solved the problem of soil erosion on the steep hills that these early gardeners were cultivating.

Though this concept of gardening hasn't really changed, the tools and equipment that we have at our disposal to make life easier certainly have. In this chapter we are going to look at some of the equipment you will definitely need, as well as some items that will just help make your gardening life that little bit less problematic. We will start with gardening tools and then we will move onto what you will need to make the raised beds themselves.

Figure 10. Retired tools.

Basic Tools:

Garden shears: Often called secateurs, this is one tool that you will use again and again and a good pair will last you a lifetime. In recent years I have watched the market get flooded with cheap shears and I can assure you that the money saved is just not worth it. There are basically two types of secateurs: the anvil type where the sharp blade meets a solid piece of metal in an almost crushing motion, and the bypass type. Bypass secateurs have two sharpened blades whose opposing faces slide past one another in the same way as a pair of scissors. These are far more effective at cutting green material whilst doing minimum damage to the plant. It is essential when cutting branches and stems that the cut remains as clean as possible. This reduces the possibility that the wound becomes infected or contaminated. Better brands can be disassembled for easier cleaning and sharpening. As you will hardly ever venture into the garden without this piece of equipment I highly recommend a holster so that it can be hung from a belt.

Gloves: Even if you are not someone who likes to wear gloves when you are working, there are times when you will need to protect your hands. I like to have two pairs of gloves. One lighter pair protects from blisters and the like when doing lighter work. The other pair are heavy welders gauntlets and they come in handy when removing brambles or pruning roses or raspberries.

Shears: Although indispensable for the ornamental garden for such jobs as shaping topiary of trimming hedges, this is one tool that does not see much use in the context of raised bed vegetable gardening so if the budget is tight, leave it at the bottom of the list.

Garden fork: You will need this for loosening soil, turning over beds and lifting compost or manure. Look for a model that is sturdy and allows you to drive it in with your foot.

Hand trowels: These are tools that you will use on an ongoing basis to dig planting holes, carved seed rows or dig out weeds. They come in all sorts of shapes and sizes. You will use it often so look for a robust one that will last a long time. A medium size will do just about anything you ask of it.

Shovel: You are going to use this guy often as well so again look for quality. For jobs like moving compost from barrow to beds, the long handled French variety work best. The shovel comes in both flat nosed and sharp nosed versions. The main thing you want it that it is capable of lifting reasonably large quantities of material such as compost or soil.

Spade: Often confused with a shovel, a spade has a flat head and is used for digging rather than scooping. Here you don't want the long handle but rather the shorter English version with a handgrip on the end which you can push with the top of your thigh for that bit of extra leverage. Because it is going to be doing some heavy duty work make sure the handle is sturdy and that its design allows for you to drive it in with your foot.

Hoes: Essentially there are two types of hoe. The traditional one has a flat blade that you drive into the ground in a short cutting motion. The other is called either a draw hoe or a stirrup hoe which you pull toward you through the top half inch or so of soil. This is great for cutting off weeds at ground level. Both have their advantages but for annual weeds that you are most likely to encounter in a raised bed, the draw hoe version will be more effective. When making your purchase make sure that you will be able to buy replacement blades.

Figure 11. Shovels are great for digging up, breaking apart and lifting soil as well as scooping and moving loose materials.

Rake: Once again there are two different types of rake. The spring tined, or lawn rake is exactly what the name suggests and won't help much in these types of beds. The ordinary garden rake comes with different sized heads. Choose a smaller size so that you can get in between plants to rake out dead material and spread mulch or top dressing.

Weeder: These are small tools designed to get in between plants and scrape out weeds. They come in all shapes and sizes and you should just choose one that suits you. Those that look like little flat bladed hoes work fine.

Trug: Trugs used to be open topped baskets made from woven wicker. Today they are more commonly made of plastic with two handles at the top. They are inexpensive and incredibly useful. I suggest buying two identical ones that fit inside one another. All the tools can be tossed into one and then the other can be used to gather weeds or crops once you harvest.

Wheelbarrow: If there is one essential item that gardeners get wrong more than any other, then in my opinion it has to be the wheelbarrow. These incredibly versatile pieces of equipment have been with us for hundreds of years since the Chinese first invented them for carrying their wounded off the battlefield. Today they come in every shape and size imaginable with folding options and two wheeled options thrown in for good measure.

Forget about what the salesman tries to sell you, this is what you need; a robust builder's barrow with one wheel at the front. Running around the front of that wheel there should be a metal bar or pipe. Don't buy it if it does not have this essential accessory. When you tip the barrow, you stand it on this metal piece and what you are carrying slides neatly where you want it to go. When you don't have it, the barrow remains balanced on its wheel which slides back toward you and hits you in the shin. It the proceeds to spread whatever you were transporting in any number of different directions.

Don't be tempted by a barrow with a solid rubber wheel and never touch one with an old metal wheel. It will sink into the soil and is ten times harder to push. Go for a heavy duty tyre with a tube. A one wheeled barrow is incredibly easy to manoeuvre and will allow you to carry a considerable amount of weight.

Figure 12. Green one wheeled barrow with a heavy duty single tyre.

There is a vast array of ancillary equipment that can be useful and which you tend to acquire along the way. Old kitchen knives are great for dividing plants and getting weeds out of paving cracks. Balls of string are always needed somewhere, and no good gardener should be without a pocket knife.

Two words of warning when it comes to tools; the first is that, as with some many other things these days, suppliers will try to sell you some sort of a gizmo or tool for just about every conceivable situation. If you believe all that the publicity suggests, you will start finding yourself wondering how you ever survived without a battery powered dibber or a corkscrew weeding tool. The truth of the matter is that we have been gardening perfectly happily without most of these gadgets for millennia so start with the items listed above and don't purchase anything else until you have identified a genuine need. When you know that you are going to use a tool then buy the best one that you can afford. Car boot sales and garage sales are a great place to acquire tools cheaply.

The second thing is that garden tools are the sneakiest things you will ever come across. Give them half a chance and they will hide in the grass or find themselves an excellent shady position to lie around in and avoid doing any work. If ever you see a gardener wandering around in aimless circles, chances are he is searching for a trowel or weeder that he had in his hand just second earlier. I have known tools to slink off and not be seen again for years until suddenly found loitering amongst the compost or in the fork of a tree. One can of brightly coloured spray paint, used liberally on wooden handles, can save you hours of pointless searching and worrying whether or not you are suffering from early-onset dementia.

Construction Basics:

Before starting actually to build your beds it would be a good idea to get everything you need in place for the job. First of all it is a good idea to decide what size beds you want and what material you want them to be made of. Here you are spoiled for choice and three distinct mindsets start to become evident. The first is the person who just wants to get started and who is willing to pay reasonably exorbitant amounts for purpose built raised beds made from hardwood and delivered as a flat pack.

The second distinct class of gardener is the perpetual recycler who believes that purchasing anything but the most essential items is somehow cheating. All of his beds tend to be made from old pallets, side panels of wrecked cars and mismatched second hand doors retrieved from a skip.

Somewhere between these two extremes is the average gardener who is prepared to buy most of what is needed but is working to a budget.

Firstly it might be a good idea to point out that none of these approaches is wrong and that the plants don't actually care. They tend to be quite un-elitist and are, for the most part, far more likely to get picky about soil conditions and climate than they are about what materials the beds are made of.

Now it is just up to you to decide which of these three categories you fall into. Raised beds can be made from any material that will support the weight of the soil and which will resist rotting in an exposed outdoor environment. Materials that work well include brick, cinder block, corrugated iron sheeting, railway sleepers and wood. Your choice will often be governed as much by what is readily available as anything else.

By far the most common material used is wood. Wood is attractive, reasonably easy to work with and most widely available. Assuming that this is the material that you want to work with, then it now only remains to work out the quantities that you will require. You need to start with the size of the beds you want and the depth. You also need to consider how to avoid as much waste as possible. I often use planks that are eight foot long, nine inches wide and two inches thick. This also just happens to be a very standard material for scaffolding boards so is a size that can be bought off the shelf at most merchants.

The reason I choose that size is that beds that are four feet wide are easy to work because they only require me to reach two feet into the bed from each side. By cutting my planks in half to obtain the end pieces I eliminate waste altogether. That means that for a bed of one plank depth, I require three boards - one for the ends and one for each side. I prefer to go a little deeper so six planks gives me eighteen inches of depth which is almost perfect.

Figure 13. Wooden raised vegetable garden beds.

Of course, the choice of wood is another matter. Standard scaffold boards tend to be made from pine which is one of the cheapest options but is not the longest lasting. Cedar lasts much longer, and though more expensive, is worth the extra investment. Rough sawn timber is cheaper than prepared wood and is perfectly acceptable for this operation. Rough sawn timber is the wood directly from the sawmill before being planed. The best way to source your timber is to order it directly from a timber yard rather than from a retail outlet. Because most yards are familiar with cutting to scaffold board size they don't need to alter their saw to accommodate your order. Just be sure that you know all of your dimensions and quantities in advance.

The price of wood varies depending on what is available in the area. In some places rough sawn hardwood such as oak can prove cheaper than softwood, so explain to the saw mill what you want to do and ask them what they suggest.

Once you have decided the size and shape of your beds you can do the calculations. Eight feet is by no means the longest length to which you can build a bed, but bear this in mind; the soil is going to put pressure on the wood and the longer you build the beds the more they are likely to bow out. It is quite easy to attach braces but you may be better off making two eight foot beds rather than one sixteen foot one. Also don't feel that you design should be limited to square or rectangular blocks. T and L shapes are not difficult to make and add further design possibilities. Just be sure to stick to sizes that make reaching across the bed easy otherwise you lose one of the major benefits of this system. Two foot is a comfortable distance to reach for the average person.

To add stability, it is common to add corner braces and one or two braces down the inside or the outside of the sides. This can be done with lengths of two by three which is another very standard timber size.

People will suggest that you use pressure treated timber, often referred to as tanalized. There is no doubt that this will add years to the life of your beds but the treatment includes a cocktail of nasty chemicals. Whilst there is no evidence that these can be transferred to the crops you are growing, it is wise practise to avoid the risk.

If you can get hold of reclaimed railway sleepers they make the most sturdy and long lasting beds. They too have been treated with bitumen but many have been exposed to weather for years. If I get them I line the inside of the bed with plastic membrane before filling so that I am sure I will get no leaching. When considering your options, understand that large timber such as sleepers requires heavy lifting and needs to be cut with a chain saw.

For most timber, a battery powered circular saw is perfect for doing your cuts and if that isn't in your tool kit then a hand cross cut saw will do the work and save you several trips to the gym. You will need suitable screws of a length two and a half times the thickness of your planks. Treated deck screws or stainless steel screws will add considerably to their longevity. If your budget extends to it you can use galvanized coach bolts instead of screws as theses are much more substantial.

Use a battery drill that doubles as a screwdriver then you just need one tool to do both jobs. Pre-drill your holes with a bit appropriate to the screws you have. You can purchase a counter sunk bit for very little and this ensures that the countersink and pre-drilling are all done in one operation.

Other tools you will definitely need are a long tape measure and a spirit level. The tape can also be used for checking for square but if you have a large builder's square this will speed that process. Don't buy one just for this job.

You now have enough equipment to build your beds. Some people like to line the inside of their beds with plastic membrane so that the wood is not always exposed to the damp soil. The problem with this system is that the water tends to sneak in between the planks and the membrane, and you then have a situation where the wood is both damp and cannot breathe. I prefer to use a non toxic penetrating wood treatment and paint all four sides of each plank with two coats.

Another individual choice is to drive corner stakes into the ground for additional strength. If the braces are in place securely this is another step that I do away with. Once the bed is squared up and filled with a couple of tons of soil it is not going to move.

You now have the basic materials for building the beds on site and you are ready for the next step. We will look at filling the completed beds in the next chapter but you are going to need good quality top soil. If you buy a bagged product and you have several beds this can soon become expensive. You are better off using loose top soil delivered as a truck load as this makes for a considerable saving. Because you cannot always rely on a speedy delivery in this situation, it is probably a good idea to order that now. Work out the volume that your beds will contain and order half of that from your local nursery or anyone else that offers good top soil. Swimming pool builders and people digging foundations often will sell a truckload at very reasonable prices. Soil is a valuable resource and if you have the place to store it then it is a wise idea to order slightly more than you think you will need. It always comes in handy somewhere.

If you are only building a very small raised bed, then garden centres sell bags of soil but in this case you won't need to buy it until we get to the next phase of the operation.

Irrigation is another option to consider as it makes your life considerably easier and reduces the amount of water that you will use. Many of the systems can be incorporated after the beds have been built but if the system you choose needs to be installed before the soil mixture going in then that too will need to be on-site before you start work. One other luxury is a greenhouse. It is undoubtedly not something that you need right away, but if you can gain access to one it will broaden your ability to grow crops and other plants over a more extended period. Book nine in this series will give you a more comprehensive look at greenhouses in general.

TOOL AND CONSTRUCTION – RECAP:

- For the garden you will mainly need hand tools
- A basic collection of hand tools will get you started. You can expand this if you need to but start small
- For construction you will need tools appropriate to the material you choose for the beds
- Beds can be made from any number of different materials according to both taste and budget
- You will need to weigh up whether or not to do the construction yourself

Figure 14. Gardening hand tool set in wicker basket

3

LOCATION AND SET-UP OF A RAISED BED GARDEN

In this chapter we are going to look at where to place your raised bed and what factors to take into account when making that decision. After that we will take a look at putting the raised bed together and the best products to use for building it and filling it.

When positioning your raised beds there is room for flexibility. It stands that you would want to try to achieve optimal placing; but that is just not always practical or possible. For instance, you can place raised beds on patios, balconies and even in greenhouses. You may not be able to achieve all of the growing criteria under these conditions, but that certainly does not mean that you should miss out on the pleasure, and benefits that gardening offers you.

Ideally, a raised bed should be placed on level ground and receive a minimum of eight hours per day of sunlight. By aligning your beds on a north south axis, you ensure that the beds receive the maximum amount of light possible. As the sun passes over from east to west the least amount of shade is given by those plants that you have in the bed. That will provide near perfect light conditions for growing most vegetables. The next crucial consideration is access to water. People often underestimate just how important this factor can be and imagine that they can just do the watering with watering cans. Carrying a heavy watering can once or twice may not seem too daunting a task, but when you have to do it twice a day for six months or more, it suddenly becomes a herculean effort. Putting an obstacle like this in your way will eventually kill your enthusiasm and place the whole project at risk. Your bed needs to be at least close enough to a tap that you can run a hosepipe to it. If you are able to trap water off the roof of your house in a water butt or tank then consider buying a small electric pump so that you can simply pump that free water to where ever it is needed.

Access is another important consideration. You will need to be able to approach the bed pushing a heavily laden wheelbarrow, so build that into your planning when choosing the final position. Ideally you would like to avoid stairs, steep slopes or overly narrow paths.

That may not be possible if you live on a slope, but there is nothing to stop you setting out your beds in a kind of terrace system with a path that winds down along the contour lines.

Of course, there are going to be situations where it is simply not possible to meet all the ideal criteria If, for example, you are putting a raised bed onto a balcony, the building will probably cause shade at some time during the day. What that may mean is that you will need to be more selective about the plants that you choose to grow. Some vegetables and herbs require less light, and then there are ornamental plants that are perfectly happy growing in shade. It is all just a question of adapting to those conditions that you cannot change.

Once you have chosen the position that offers you the best conditions for your raised beds, it is time to do some planning. This is the step that so many people either skim over or miss out altogether. People are keen to get on with the job and start moving forward as soon as possible. I believe it is for this reason that we see so many vegetable gardens that are purely functional but lack aesthetic appeal, and it really isn't necessary. A vegetable garden can be a thing of great beauty and raised beds enhance that because the plants are much closer to eye level than in lower beds. You may choose to go down the purely functional route, and that is fine, but don't go there just because you were in too much of a hurry to spend a few hours planning.

First of all, measure out the area that will become your vegetable garden. There is no need for extreme accuracy so you can probably just pace it out. Once you have done that, do a scale drawing on an A4 piece of paper and then just do some sketches and experiments to see what your options are. There are some templates at the end of this book and for more visual inspiration, take a browse through some garden magazines and surf the internet a little. An excellent way to get inspiration is to visit some of the better known public gardens where you will see design used in inspirational ways. When you have seen just what can be achieved with well designed raised bed gardens, you will be glad that you took the extra time.

Another factor to take into account is that garden design is beginning to change because of changing global weather. There is a move away from the large rolling lawns of the past. This space is now being turned over to water wise planting and productive beds like the ones you are considering, where both soil and water can be better managed. Over the next few decades, though it is likely that lawns will not disappear altogether, their dominance of the landscape will be far more restricted. It is often the lawn that demands most in terms of maintenance time, chemicals and water. All of this to produce what is, in nature's terms, just a vast area of monoculture that is not conducive to any form of biodiversity. Design is an important aspect to all garden preparation and in book seven in this series we will be going into the design process at greater length.

In your design consider different shapes of bed as well as combining them with other garden features such as flower beds, ponds and nice seating areas. Why should your raised bed garden be purely functional when, with no extra cost, you can turn it into a visual oasis that just happens to produce wonderful healthy food? One advantage of a well thought out design is that you can grow into it. You may not immediately be able to put in all of those raised beds, or that pond of your dreams, but if it is on your drawing and you have planned for it, it can be added later. Because you already know where it will go, the design will be cohesive and not just a higgildy piggildy mess where each addition looks like the after thought that it was.

Remember when drawing up your design to consider access. Beds should not be more than four feet wide. If you build up against a fence or wall, narrow the bed width to two feet as you won't be able to access both sides of the bed. That doesn't mean that you are restricted to squares and rectangles. Throw in some T shapes or right angle turns. Even a U shaped bed can be both practical and attractive. Changing the height of the beds can also add another pleasing design dimension. This is a chance to be daring and stamp your signature on a garden that may well be with you for many years. You are no longer obliged to follow the dull rectangular layout that our ancestors used. Instead you can go a little wild whilst still remaining within the boundaries of practicality.

Paths need to be carefully considered too, when drawing up your plan. Never make paths narrower than the width of a wheel barrow and if you can make them a little wider to aid manoeuvrability then do so. You are going to be using those paths regularly, so you don't want them turning into muddy quagmires. That entails typically surfacing them with something. This need not be expensive. The timber yard where you bought your wood may well be quite happy to get rid of those wood chips that they create in such abundance. Other options include gravel, broken roof tiles and building rubble. I have even worked in a garden where there were so many stones that I could just grab a few bucketfuls of them as I worked and cast them along the pathways as I went along. Eventually they gave me a wonderful gravel path and for free while at the same time loosening up the soil in the beds. Again, the choice of materials is related to your budget and if you have a substantial one you could consider paving or concreting those areas that you will be walking along so frequently. Concrete is labour intensive but leaves you with a long lasting and solid path. Again, with a little thought and ingenuity, even a plain concrete path can be transformed into something attractive. Both brushed concrete and pebble mosaic techniques are easy to master and make cheap aesthetic additions.

Once you are happy with your design, it is time to start putting it all together. The first thing you will need to do is to take a good look at the ground on which you will be placing the bed. If it is grassy then you will have to lift the turf before you start. Unfortunately this can be a bit of a back breaking job. The best way to tackle this task is with a sharp spade, cutting underneath the turf and lifting spade sized pieces off to expose the bare earth underneath. Set these sods aside as they will come in useful at a later stage. If the chosen plot is covered in weeds then these can simply be pulled out by hand. Don't waste them either. They will make a great start for the compost heap that you will eventually create. You will discover as you venture deeper into this subject, that gardeners are highly adept at reusing all sorts of materials that most people wouldn't have considered. If you are time rich and don't intend to start building the garden immediately, you can cover the ground with black plastic sheeting and the grass and weeds will weaken considerably due to light deprivation. When you need to clear them, the task will be that much simpler.

Once you have cleared the ground where the raised bed is to be placed, dig it over to a depth of about six inches using a garden fork. This is simply to maximize drainage. After that rake it over lightly, and then you can lay your spirit level on it in a couple of places and see that it is level. If it is not, it may be that you are easily able to achieve a level simply by raking some soil from the higher patches to the lower ones. If the incline is more serious then you will need to dig down the higher ground until a level can be achieved. The reason that level ground is essential is that soil in a sloped bed will put greater pressure on the lower walls of the bed and that will reduce their lifespan.

At this point, it is probably a good time to look at the different options that are available to you from which to build your project. Much will depend on what materials are readily available, your skill levels and the time you have. Permanent structures made from brick or cinder block both work well. You will need to cast a concrete foundation and wait for it to set but it doesn't have to be very deep as you are unlikely to be building to a height of more than two feet. Working with bricks and blocks requires different tools to woodwork and you will need to get the hang of basic brick laying, as well as purchasing sand, stone and cement.

If you are near a quarry or have access to quantities of stone, this too can give you an attractive bed that will last a long time. Stone walls can be held together using cement or they can be dry stone walls.

Wood is probably the most commonly used material in raised bed building. Eventually it does rot, but if you use a good timber like cedar and you treat it with a non-toxic preservative you are likely to get many years of service from each bed.

Other materials include woven willow or wattle. This is an easy to use material if you have access to it. Stakes are driven into the ground every 12 inches and then lengths of the weaving material are simply threaded between them in a basket weave manner. This is a very attractive option that was widely used in the medicinal gardens of European monasteries during the Middle Ages. Such beds can be built up to a height of two feet, which is generally as deep as you would need your beds to be. The product does not have a very long life span and you should not bank on getting more than three or four seasons from it. The inside can be lined with a plastic membrane or landscape fabric which will reduce drainage through the sides and help increase the life span of the bed.

Railway sleepers are long lasting, attractive and provide a really solid bed that will last for years. Used railway sleepers are becoming harder to source these days, but there are now timber companies that have recognized this gap in the market. They have turned to cutting sleeper sized timbers with gardeners in mind, and they often sell their produce through garden centres. Whilst they are not strictly true railway sleepers, they offer the same advantages without the bitumen products that were used in the original preservation process. Disadvantages are that there will be some heavy duty lifting involved in the construction process and unless you have a really big circular saw they will need to be cut with a chain saw. They will also be pricey, so you will need to decide if their longevity outweighs the cost. If you can overcome the down side, you will have a wonderful bed that will serve you well for many years.

Plastic planks are a relatively new possibility. Produced using recycled plastic, these boards can be screwed onto wooden or even metal, posts in the same way as wooden boards would be. This is a long lasting option but you will need to install support posts at regular intervals as they tend to bow under pressure. This is not a huge effort and if you can access this material at a reasonable price, then it is one that you may want to consider.

Another possibility using plastic is a fit together kit that you assemble yourself. These take the form of blocks that clip together, a little like a child's Lego kit. Being plastic they will last for many years but unless the designers have made some changes recently, they tend to bow out at the joints due to the soil pressure. The colour range is also quite limited and tends to be a little incongruous with the natural finish that most people would hope for in a garden. That may well improve as use of this product expands. They clip together really quickly and you can have your bed up in just a couple of hours.

There are also pre-made wooden kits that you assemble yourself and which are made from red cedar. These are delivered as a flat pack. Though not cheap, they are easy to assemble and they eliminate the use of tools such as the circular saw. Some manufacturers will produce these to your dimensions so that you can choose the design rather than being dictated to by limited shapes and sizes.

The final option is to hire a professional to build the beds for you. All landscapers will be familiar with this sort of work and have the requisite tools. Most of them are familiar with garden design so they could help you from that aspect as well. If you are choosing wood, and there is not a landscaper available, then it is easily within the scope of any carpentry company.

Obviously, there will be extra costs if you are hiring outside professionals. You will need to decide for yourself whether having the job done so that you can focus on the gardening aspect warrants that expense. Many people these days suffer from time poverty and this may be the quickest way forward for them.

Finally there is the recycled bits and pieces option. I have seen beds made with woven pieces of cast off hosepipe, sand bags, recovered fishing nets, old doors and driftwood. With a little artistic wizardry, any number of materials can be used. The point here is not so much what you make your beds with, but the fact that this system is so flexible. As long as what you are using can contain the weight of damp soil, and is non-toxic, it can be used for this purpose.

Despite the vast array of options, most beds will be made from planks. They are attractive to the eye, widely accessible and fairly easy to convert into raised beds. Most of the assembly work only requires a minimum of carpentry know how, and the average home handyman will cope easily. Whatever route you choose to go down, be aware that the soil does exert a lot of pressure and the beds need to be strong enough to support that. A simple brace, screwed firmly down from one side of the bed to the other will often be all that is needed to prevent the planks from bowing outwards. A more attractive option is to attach a top frame. This is a wooden frame that is fastened to the top of the bed but with the planks laid flat rather than on their sides. The frame needs only to be about four inches wide so you can just split some of the same size boards that you used for the sides up the middle using your circular saw. Because the top frame is flat it adds considerable strength while at the same time giving a nicely finished appearance to your creation.

Figure 15. Cedar is usually the best wood to use for garden beds because it is naturally rot resistant.

Once your beds are made and in position, check them for square. Beds of this size easily distort. You can either use a builders setting out square or a tape measure for this job. Measure diagonally from corner to corner and once you are getting the same size measurement across both diagonals, then your bed is square. If they are out of square don't be too concerned. As long as your dimensions were all cut to the correct size then you will be able to get them to square up with a little prodding and gentle persuasive kicking. If they aren't strong enough to sustain a bit of nudging at this stage, they won't cope with the wait that the growing medium will exert on them later.

PRE-PLANNING AND POSITIONING – RECAP:

- Consider the position and the slope of the ground
- Aim to position the beds to run from north to south where feasible
- Consider access to water and distance from the house or shed
- Focus on a design before doing any work. The garden does not have to be purely functional
- Consider the materials available and what works best for you. Wood, stone, brick, railway sleepers, woven willow and plastic are all options as are reclaimed materials
- Bear in mind the soil will put pressure on the sides
- Consider size of paths and materials they could be made from

4

FILLING THE BEDS

F inally, your design is finished, your plot is cleared and your bed frames assembled. It is now time to start filling your beds so that you can get down to growing some crops. The success of your harvest depends on what you now do. You might scrimp and save on the frame of the beds but the growing medium is essential. Firstly decide if you need to lay a mesh into the bottom of your beds. You will do this if you suspect that mice, moles or other rodents are going to try to enter from ground level.

Next decide if you are going to need to place a membrane to slow the drainage of water. You will only need to do this if you are on really sandy soil and you will have been easily able to deduce this while you were preparing the ground. Some people like to use a weed proof membrane to stop unwanted plants taking advantage of the beautiful growing conditions and suddenly making an appearance in their carefully laid out planting scheme. If your beds are deep, this is unlikely to happen. Weeds that attempt to grow through two feet of soil are unlikely to make it to the surface, and even if they do, they will be in such a weakened state that they will be easy to deal with. In shallower beds, it is possible that some weeds will make their way to the surface and so some sort of a membrane will prevent this. You can purchase weed proof membrane from most garden centres. This allows water to penetrate but prevents plants from doing so. Many gardeners simply layer the bottom of their beds with old sheets of corrugated cardboard made by flattening boxes. These are free and will break-down eventually, but by then any resident weeds will have almost definitely have died.

If you feel you need to line the sides of the beds with a waterproof membrane then now is the time to do so. You can purchase heavy duty plastic from most builders' merchants and this can simply be stapled to the insides of the bed with a good industrial stapler. Once the soil is added it will hold the liner in place effectively. Pond liners are another option but they are usually more expensive.

Once you have decided which of these options to go for and fitted the relevant materials, you are free to start putting in the bottom layer. This is the drainage layer and you have a wide choice of options available. You can purchase gravel but although it will do the job it will need to be delivered and it costs money. If you prefer the free option, then you can use old sticks, brush, grass clippings or even small logs. In short, that bottom layer can consist of any organic material that is free draining as your plants will be growing in the layer above. This is a great time to get rid of those sods that you dug up and put aside. They can be turned upside down and laid back into the bed grass and all. After that just stomp them flat and lay in whatever layer is going in next.

A brief warning when filling the bottom layer; use composed or semi composed plant matter. Lawn clippings are a good example. Once they have started to break down and formed almost a compost themselves, they are ideal for the bottom of raised beds. The breaking down process of green material uses nitrogen, so if you throw in large amounts of green matter such as lawn or hedge clippings, it will deplete the layer above of this important plant nutrient. After just a few weeks those clipping will have broken down enough to no longer to pose a threat in this way. This means the green clippings will need to have been composted or you will need to allow the material to break down in the beds before adding the soil.

It is the top twelve inches of your new beds where all the action is going to take place and this is where you want your soil to be in peak condition. There is any number of recipes out there for you to try but this one will stand you in good stead. Aim for forty percent homemade garden compost, forty percent soil and twenty percent sharp sand. Many people tend to over-complicate this process and it really doesn't need to be too complicated at all. Soil is a living, breathing, organism that we all too often overlook. As you become more involved in the process of gardening you will begin to see it as your most precious resource. Throughout this series of books you will pick up tips on how to enhance the condition of your soil. If your soil is not healthy then your plants won't be healthy. Much of the agricultural industry has so degraded their soil that they can no longer grow crops without adding vast amounts of chemical fertilizer. As an organic gardener you won't want to go down that slippery path, and proper soil management is the only way to avoid it.

The compost is high in nutrients, especially if manure was used in the process of making it. I always include some form of manure when making compost because it provides me with that high nutrient level that my plants need. It will help to feed the plants and it acts like a sponge at the same time, so it will help retain moisture. The sand is simply to ensure that things don't get clogged up and that drainage remains free flowing. What you are aiming for is a dark crumbly mix that feels slightly damp and cool.

This is one of the cheapest ways to fill your beds. If you were unable to purchase top soil, or if it was prohibitively expensive, you might be able to scrape the top layer from what will now become your paths. It is only wasted where it is at the moment and so you can shovel it up and toss it into the beds and then replace it with an easy to walk on material like wood chips. Often your topsoil will include some garden weed seeds. They will generally sprout quickly and be easy to deal with by hand. If you are unfortunate enough to have lots of weeds then you may have to revert to covering the soil with black plastic for a fortnight once it is in the bed. This will weaken any seeds that survive.

The compost that you use should be well broken down and you may need to buy it if you don't already have some. As soon as you start gardening, one of the first things you will be doing is making your own compost so in future you should be able to top up beds from your own supply. If you have access to well rotted manure then you can augment the mix with that. Halve the amount of compost and replace it with the manure. A word of warning about manure; if it is still fresh it can burn your plants so set it aside for a few months until it has time to mature. Most farmers have plenty of manure and they can often be persuaded to drop you off a trailer load. If you have this option, then grab it even if you can't use the manure immediately. It is one of those resources that gardeners can never have too much of. Don't worry if it comes with loads of straw in it. It all just adds to the cocktail that your plants will delight in. Well rotted manure does not smell bad, contrary to public opinion.

Fill the beds until the contents are literally bulging out over the top and then let everything sit for around two weeks. Fairly quickly you will notice the whole heap beginning to subside as it settles into its new home. What you have done is created a perfect environment in which plants will thrive. Over time the materials in the bed will continue to subside though not at the same rate as they did over the first fortnight. Don't be alarmed at this. It is part of the natural decomposition process and you will be regularly adding to it to keep it in perfect condition.

Figure 16. Filling a newly constructed raised bed with soil.

There are many other recipes for filling the beds, and one which you will see often replaces the compost with peat. There are places in Canada where peat is being produced by nature faster than it can be harvested, but in much of the rest of the world, and certainly in the United Kingdom and Europe, peat extraction is not sustainable and is causing severe environmental problems, including releasing methane gas into the atmosphere. There are alternatives such as coconut Coir and rice husks which are bi-products of the agricultural industry. Still, as gardening starts to grow from a hobby into an obsession, you will find that more and more of what you need can be obtained from your own resources. You will be producing your own compost and gathering fallen leaves to make leaf mould. Soon buying things like Coir will mostly become a thing of the past.

If you can resist the urge to start growing things in your new beds immediately, then letting them sit for a fortnight or even longer, is a good idea. Another thing that you can do is to test your soil so that you know precisely how acid or alkaline it is. This can be done by sending a sample to a laboratory or by using a home testing kit. Ideally you want to have a PH of six to seven, which is ideal for growing most vegetables. In the regions of five to eight should not see plant growth being inhibited in any way. Although it may be comforting to test your soil, correcting it can be costly and often involves the use of chemical additives. As you are mixing the growing medium yourself, you are sure that all the ingredients are natural and it is highly unlikely that it will fall outside of the above PH levels. With experience, you will reach a point where you can judge whether a soil will provide an excellent growing medium just by picking up a handful and rolling it around in your hand.

Figure 17. Perfect soil.

" You have to take the time to prepare the soil
if you want to embrace the seeds".
- William P. Young.

FILLING THE BEDS – RECAP:

- Before starting to fill, decide if you want to line the sides or place a mesh against rodents such as moles
- The top thirty centimetres are the most important. The lower section can be filled with most vegetable materials as it will break down eventually
- Think about drainage
- Buy good soil and mix it with good ameliorants such as compost or well-rotted manure
- Try to let filled beds sit for a fortnight before planting
- Test your soil if you are not sure of its quality

5

WHAT TO PLANT WHEN

This is the part of the process that you have probably been looking most forward to. After all that effort, you are now at a point where you can decide what plants you want to grow and what methods best suit your situation. Should you plant seeds directly into the soil or should they be started in trays? Should you be starting out with seeds or would you be better off with seedlings? More importantly, what plants should you choose?

The last question is probably the easiest to answer so we will begin there. The best vegetables to grow are those that you eat on a daily basis. An excellent place to start is with your weekly shopping list. Items that are most likely to appear are onions, tomatoes, lettuce and beans. After that you probably buy the odd cabbage, carrots and peas. All of these make good choices for your planting plan and that planting plan is crucial. Potatoes are another staple of our diets but I will get to that as some alternative methods can save you time and space.

Figure 18. Many varieties of beans are considered the easiest vegetables to grow for beginners gardeners.

Draw to scale an outline plan of your beds. You probably have this already from when you laid out your design. You will want to make several photocopies of this and perhaps consider some sort of file that you can keep them in. Onto this plan you will mark what crops are going in and when. You will also be able to give a rough estimate of when you hope to harvest so that you know what space will become available for either a second sowing of the same crop or a different crop. Each season you will fill out a new plan and make adjustments according to how successful certain crops were, how much excess you had and any problems that you encountered. If, like me, you are not the greatest record keeper, this may seem a little long winded and unnecessary. Over the years I have learned that records are crucial to improving my results and making me a better gardener. I keep both a daily diary and the garden plans that I worked on in previous years. With these I am able to look back and see what cultivars and varieties worked most effectively, what pests or diseases I encountered and even what the weather patterns were like. As you build up this catalogue of records you will start to become more effective at choosing your crops at the start of the season. I start my gardening day by going through the diary of that date during previous years and almost invariably it reminds me of some chore that I should be doing or something that I should be adding to my planting list. I now have records going back ten years and it is difficult to overstate their importance. Gardening requires such a wide variety of different tasks to be performed by the gardener that it is easy to overlook something that may later turn out to have been important. Record-keeping helps build up a catalogue of things to be done and plants that worked or didn't work.

The more comprehensive you make your records, the more valuable they will be. Each year you will visit plant markets and nurseries and have catalogues drop into your letterbox. At first, you will be like a child let loose in a sweet shop. There will be so many choices available to you that it will be difficult to make up your mind. The temptation to try out that exotic new tomato, that strange-looking pepper or that different coloured potato, will be almost overwhelming. I am not suggesting that you should ever lose that sense of wonder and excitement. Every year a portion of my planting plan is dedicated to exotic experiments. Some have been a delight and others a total wipe out. It is only through record-keeping that I am able to keep track of the stalwarts - the plants that I know are going to cope with local conditions and produce a reliable crop season after season. The produce I grow is an integral part of what goes onto my table and I can't afford the time, effort and expense of too many failed experiments. Unfortunately, the nursery industry has become as cutthroat as any other, and there is always competition to come up with the next new idea and the next so-called wonder plant. Very often they don't live up to the sales hype that accompanies them and, whilst it may be novel to have a black tomato on your plate, if it tastes watery or bland you may be disappointed.

Another thing that you will discover is that many of the seed companies are owned by the same handful of large corporations who dominate much of the industry. They patent their seeds and cross-breed in search of the new wonder variety of the year, but often you will not be able to harvest your own seed from the crop because they do not come true to form on a second sowing. These seeds are known as F1 hybrids. Many of these F1 varieties will produce a very good harvest the first year and it is by keeping good records that you will know whether to purchase new seed and sow the same crop the following year.

One real positive advance over recent years has been that of the heirloom seed movement. These are people who specialize in and are passionate about, reintroducing seeds that have gone out of fashion. It is here, that you are most likely to rediscover those old fashioned tomatoes that your grandmother used to grow or that runner bean that seems impossible to locate anymore. These crops may lack the perfect aesthetic appeal that many supermarket crops have, but they will more than make up for it in terms of taste and shelf life. What is more is that you will be able to harvest your own seed for free and repeat the results in years to come. Many gardening clubs support the heirloom seed movement and I cannot stress how valuable these clubs are, both as a source of information and as a place at which to swap seeds, seedlings and even some of your excess harvest.

The reason that antique seeds have become so rare is that seed companies stopped promoting them. There were two reasons for this. One was that the demand for perfect looking vegetables grew as people left the land and moved to cities. The companies simply responded to that demand. Once people lost their connection with the land, they came to assume that a misshapen vegetable was not as good to eat as perfectly looking one. This has resulted in huge amounts of food waste as perfectly edible vegetables are thrown away, simply because they failed to meet the aesthetic requirements of the supermarkets and their clients. This, in turn, has led to another movement called the ugly vegetable movement which is trying to persuade buyers to purchase these slightly deformed crops.

Food that is not perfect looking is no less nutritious than that is. In fact, the opposite is often true. Vegetables are bred for form and colour rather than taste, as the supermarkets realized that people made their purchases based primarily on what they saw. Gradually we have come to believe that gnarled carrots or misshapen tomatoes are not as tasty or are inferior in some way. When breeding plants for a specific requirement, such as how they look, we often lose other benefits in the breeding process and it is frequently taste that is forfeited first. When we start going back to non-hybrid seed, we generally regain some of the qualities that were once taken for granted.

The second reason non modified seed fell out of use was that seed companies discovered that if they made minor adjustments to a plant, either through cross-breeding or genetic modification, then they were able to take out a patent on that seed. Obviously, there were higher profits to be made on seed to which they owned sole rights, and gradually the unpatented seed just fell from our collective memories. It was simply not subjected to the massive marketing tactics applied to patented crops.

Because seeds are often the cheapest way to grow vegetables, and because they offer a natural place to begin, we will start by looking at growing some of your plants from seed. Some seeds remain viable for decades and others won't last for long. There are

Figure 19. Many vegetables, annuals, herbs and perennials sprout easily from seed sown directly into garden soil.

even examples of botanists being able to grow plants from seed found in Egyptian pyramids while parsnips grow best from seed that is fresh. When purchasing packets of seed, you almost always end up with more seed than you can use in a single sowing. Gardeners cannot throw away seed. It is simply genetically impossible for someone who grows plants to throw these valuable little life sources into the garbage. The result is that if you are not careful, you will end up with a vast collection of seed. As a rule of thumb don't plant seed that is older than three years and always label and date stored seed clearly. Keep it in a plastic box such as a used ice cream container and store it in a dark cupboard. One advantage of associating with other gardeners is that you can share or swap seeds and thus avoid the trauma of deciding what to do with all that excess that you inevitably acquire. This also means that you naturally start to build variety into your planting.

Some seed comes coated in clay to allow for easier handling and others come embedded into a degradable paper strip so all that the gardener needs to do is to lay the strip into a drill and cover it with soil. When the plants finally appear, they will be perfectly evenly spaced. Seeds are either sown in situ or are germinated in a protected environment and then planted out as more hardy seedlings.

Rather than go into the different methods on a general basis, we will start to look at some of the more commonly grown plants individually and this will give you a more practical approach that you can then use more widely. In this book, we will focus on those plants that are grown by almost all gardeners. In the next book of advanced techniques, we will delve more deeply into less common crops that add that little bit more adventure, both to the cultivation and to your dining table. It is here that the whole process starts to become a little addictive.

Figure 20. Spring greens under the sun's rays.

TOMATOES

Although not a true vegetable, we won't get bogged down in botanical classification and in this instance, we will treat them as one. Tomatoes are one of the most widely eaten vegetable crops and part of the reason for this is that they can be used for such a variety of culinary purposes. You will find them as important ingredients in everything from salads to sauces and pizzas to jams.

There is a huge variety of sizes, shapes, colours and tastes to choose from and, to be honest, most of what is on offer in the regular supermarket is merely a bland tip of a very large iceberg. Of all the vegetables that you will produce, few can match the taste of a fresh tomato picked directly from the vine and popped straight into your mouth while still warm from the sun. Tomatoes can also be expensive, so growing your own makes economic sense.

I won't even dare suggest what varieties you should choose as that would be like offering you fashion guidance having never met you. I would recommend that if you have contact with any local gardeners in your area that you ask some suggestions. Some cultivars will do better in one area than another and I have never met a gardener who is not happy to share knowledge of this kind. Just be prepared to spend a while listening once they get started.

There are three basic forms of tomato plant. The indeterminate can grow to 2.5 meters in height. Semi-determinates are shorter and then there are bush varieties that can be as small as 25 centimetres. Taller varieties will need to be securely staked, especially if they bear large fruit like the 'Coeur de Boeuf' or the 'Beefsteak'. I would suggest growing at least three different varieties.

Figure 21. Tomato seedling transplanted into a raised bed.

When you place them on your planting plan be sure to take the height and size into account so that they are not casting too much shade on your other crops. In general, this would mean putting them at the northern end of your beds when growing in the northern hemisphere.

In warm climates, tomato seeds can be sown directly into the ground in drills as soon as the last frosts have passed. A drill is a gardening term for a narrow trench into which the seeds are laid before being covered with soil. Gardeners love obscure terms like this because it makes us sound far more skilled and intellectual and the term shallow trenches doesn't have the same impact. An easy way to make straight drills for your beds is to first rake it over until the soil forms a nice crumbly tilth (another highly professional term that shows you know what you are talking about). Next, cut a piece of cane the width of the interior of the bed. You press this firmly down into the soil and it leaves you a perfectly formed and straight narrow trench (drill) to drop your seeds into. Tomato seeds are small so cover them with no more than a centimetre of soil, firm it down gently and water with a fine spray. A few days later, as if by a miracle, small green leaves will start to fight their way through the soil. You will need to thin these out so that the plants are evenly spaced in accordance with whatever variety you have chosen to plant. There will be instructions as to what planting distance to use printed on the seed packet.

I prefer to start my tomatoes indoors so that I get an early head start on the season and because I am too impatient to wait for the winter to end before I start gardening. Six weeks before the last frosts, I sow seed into a seed tray or plastic ice cream box with holes poked through the bottom. (Ice cream boxes are a bit of a recurring theme and good gardening requires large scale consumption of this product). Fill the box or tray with seed or cutting compost. This is a mixture that contains little or no nutrients which can rot the seed. All it does is retain moisture and provide a substrate for the seed to root into. The seed itself contains enough energy reserves in the form of starch, to get the seedling kicked off. Sprinkle the seed onto the seed compost and then lightly cover it with a thin layer of the same compost. The easiest way to do this is to place some compost into a sieve and then shake it gently over the seed tray until the seeds are just covered.

When the plantlets produce their first set of true leaves, you can gently lift them from the seed tray and plant them into individual pots containing potting soil. Lift the plants by their leaves and not by the stems which will still be very fragile. These pots need only be small and a four to six-centimetre diameter is quite large enough. Keep the soil slightly damp and place containers on a sunny window sill or in a frost free cold frame or greenhouse. As spring draws nearer you can start placing the seedlings outdoors during the day and bringing them in again at night in a process known as hardening off. This speeds their growth and allows them to gradually adapt to their final growing conditions rather than suddenly exposing them at the last minute, which could result in losses due to shock.

By the time the first frosts have passed, the seedlings will already be about 15 to 20 centimetres high and they can be planted at the correct spacing directly into your new bed. If the plants are not of the bush variety, you will need to provide suitable stakes before you plant. You are now officially a gardener and can start wearing one of those peculiar hats that are a pre-requisite of the trade. Plants should be watered weekly but do not overwater as this creates the risk of all sorts of diseases and reduces the taste. The official suggestion is that each adult plant should receive about ten litres per week. An easier approach is to stick your finger into the soil at the base of the plant and see that it is still slightly damp. If the plant is suffering water stress it will tell you by looking wilted. Learning to read the condition of your plants will eventually prove far more reliable than measuring out exact quantities of water.

I am a great believer in mulch and will go into greater detail on this subject in the next chapter. Mulch is any material laid on the soil that inhibits weed growth and helps retain water. Compost makes an excellent mulch for tomatoes as they are heavy feeders. Spread a five-centimetre layer around the base of the plants but not touching the actual stem. If mulch piles up against the base of the stem it can induce rotting. The mulch will dramatically increase moisture retention while at the same time slowly leaching nutrients down to the hungry roots.

Plants will now start to grow rapidly and taller varieties will need to be tied into their stakes regularly. Pinch out all side shoots when they are three-centimetre long and as summer draws to a close pinch out the top shoot two shoots above the topmost trusses. This will mean that the plant focuses all of its growth and nutrition on the fruit rather than on continuing to try to get taller. Fruits can be harvested when ripe, but if you live in a colder area then there may still be unripe fruit on the plant as the first frosts approach. To ensure you get all the fruit to ripen, gently bend the stems over onto some straw and cover the plants with a light horticultural fleece or clear plastic sheeting. The plant will continue to grow long enough for those last fruits to be harvested.

Figure 22. Learn to love your imperfect organic fruit and vegetables.

ONIONS

Onions are another vegetable whose value in the kitchen we sometimes fail to recognize. Onions are a simply wonderful vegetable to grow because they are a hugely versatile culinary ingredient, often being used in conjunction with tomatoes. Another really great advantage that onions bring is their longevity. Even if you grow a great deal of them, they can be stored quite easily, and a good crop could well see you right through the winter.

Onions can be grown either from seed or from sets. Sets are simply small Onions that were grown and harvested, before ripening during the previous season. Sow seed in early spring in drills to a depth of one centimetre. In a raised bed you can keep your rows about 20-centimetres apart. Planting in the ground will require greater spacing but the raised beds guarantee soil quality and ease of access for harvesting so you can tighten up a little.

Sow the seed thinly and then thin the seedlings as the leaves begin to appear. You might need to do this in stages, but ideally, you want to get to a point where each plant is about 10 centimetres from its neighbour. You may be able to keep them more closely bunched if you are growing smaller varieties. There will be a suggested planting distance on the packet. If you choose to use sets then you can plant them at their requisite spacing at the beginning of spring. Plant them to a depth where just the tips appear above the surface of the soil. Sets cost more than seed does but they give you a valuable jump start in much the same way that using seedling does. In the case of both seeds and sets, the price to return ratio is so broad that you don't really need to consider it. Even if you only get to harvest a small percentage of the crop earlier, that will more than offset the extra cost.

Once established, onions need little watering except in conditions of very dry weather. One problem you may have when using sets is that blackbirds sometimes pull them up. I am not sure why they engage in this act of horticultural vandalism but I suspect that they are convinced the set hides some edible treat. Cover them with netting until they mature a little and you will easily overcome this issue. The blackbirds may make a nuisance of themselves from time to time but they are valuable allies in the war against slugs and snails.

Figure 23. Harvested homegrown onions and carrots in wicker basket.

Before storing your crop, wait until the leaves die back naturally. The bulbs can then be lifted with a fork and they should be allowed to dry thoroughly. Usually, you can just leave them on the ground for about ten days in order to do this. If the weather is wet then hang them up indoors in netting bags of the type in which you buy oranges. Once the outside layer of skin has turned to a dry parchment they are ready to be stored. They still need to be handled with care as any bruises may lead to rotting. You can continue to store them in netting bags after cutting off the dead leaves or you can plait them using their leaves. Leave them in a cool dark place with plenty of air circulation and they should last for months.

LETTUCE

Lettuce are low growing leafy annuals that can come in a variety of colours ranging from green through to red, and which have leaves that range from smooth to indented and curly. Some cultivars form tight hearts and others have no heart at all. We are all familiar with these plants as they are an almost essential ingredient of many salads in the summer months. It is up to you to choose which variety you prefer but you might like to bear this in mind. Salad wilts quite quickly making it very difficult to store. If you go for a loose leafed variety with no heart such as 'Salad Bowl' or 'Lolo Rossa' then you can cut just enough of the outside leaves for your daily needs and leave the plant in the ground. The plant will continue to produce new leaves and in this way, you prolong the harvest period and overcome the storage problem. Another advantage is that lettuces are prone to what is known as bolting. This is a situation where they grow upwards and become bitter as they rush to produce seed. Those varieties that don't have hearts are less prone to doing this.

Lettuce plants prefer cooler weather and growing conditions of between 10 and 20°C are ideal, especially if you have cooler evenings. In cooler climates, it is possible to grow these plants in succession by sowing at two to three-week intervals so that you always have a crop ready to harvest throughout the growing season which runs from spring to late summer. You may be able to grow a longer succession of lettuce, even in warmer areas, if you place them under hoops and cover it with shade cloth. Hoops are accessories that are really easy to use in raised beds.

Sow hardy varieties in the early part of autumn. You can let these overwinter and harvest them in the spring. A plastic floating mulch thrown over the top of the plants will protect them but still allow them room to grow. A floating mulch is a perforated lightweight plastic sheeting that you lay over the plants and just tuck into the soil leaving enough room that the plants can gently lift the plastic as they grow. Sow seeds in drills between 1 and 2 centimetres deep and when the first plants appear thin them to around seven centimetres. You will need to thin them again in early spring but if you suffered any losses you can easily fill the gaps with some of the thinnings. You can also plant some of these into another bed. If you live in an area that experiences heavy snow or frost then overwintering lettuce outdoors is unlikely to be successful.

More heat resistant varieties can be sown directly in early spring. They grow quickly so they will appear in just over a week. Successive planting extends the growing period but these are hard plants to grow during the hot summer months. To further extend the growing period you can sow them in trays six weeks before the last frost and then plant them out as soon as frosts have cleared. Because these seedlings are so heat adverse, it is best to plant them out in the late afternoon and water them in so that their roots remain cool and they are not too stressed as they adjust to their new home. I am a great proponent of starting plants early indoors and then planting out the seedlings as soon as the last chance of frost has passed. This requires plenty of windowsill space or a heated greenhouse. For hardier vegetables, you can use your hoops to make a little mini greenhouse in one of your raised beds and so get a jump start when the spring arrives.

Lettuce roots should always be damp but never water-logged. This makes a raised bed the ideal place in which to cultivate them. As with tomatoes, they will tell you if they need water by wilting and providing you have been observant, you should have time to revive them. If they do start to look a little frazzled, then just sprinkle them with water even if it is during the heat of the day. Although watering in the heat of the day is regarded as the wrong thing to do when gardening, lettuce can wilt so quickly that you can afford to break the rules in this instance. These are one plant that will benefit from some of the shade that your taller tomatoes may offer, so bear that in mind when drawing up your planting plan.

Loose leaf varieties normally take around seven weeks to harvest though if you are cutting off just a few leaves from each plant you can start doing this as soon as the leaves are large enough. Other varieties, such as the 'Crispheads' and 'Cos', which have a more structured heart need to be harvested as soon as they reach maturity. If you leave them in the ground for too long then they will bolt.

Figure 24. Homegrown lettuce is more nutritious and flavourful than anything you will find at the grocery store.

BEANS

Green beans are a crop that offer many advantages to the home gardener because they are easy to store even when there is a bumper harvest. The range of beans that you can grow is huge. Beans are divided roughly into two types, those with edible pods and those whose pods must be removed before eating. We are going to look at two types of Soft Shelled Bean, the Bush Bean and the Runner Bean, which is sometimes called a Pole Bean. Both are very happy to be cultivated in raised beds and there is just something about a neat row of well trained runner beans that makes a vegetable garden look classically ornate.

Both these types of bean are warm weather beans so don't try to sow them until you are sure that the last of the frosts is past. Unless the soil has had time to warm up a little they simply won't germinate.

Sow Bush Beans in drills at a depth of about two centimetres with rows about forty centimetres apart. This is a lot closer than with a standard bed but in the raised beds you will be able to harvest them more easily so you can afford to crowd them a little. Plant seeds fifteen centimetres apart.

They will be ready to harvest in seven to eight weeks and will go on producing for a further two to three weeks. This means that if you sow a succession of seeds every three weeks, you can extend your harvest season right up until the first frosts. They are deep rooted so don't try to grow them in containers and then plant them out as success will be minimal.

Figure 25. The joy of harvesting fresh vegetables in your own garden.

Your runner beans can grow to a height of two and a half meters so you will need to supply a structure of at least this height to support them. That support needs to last through the whole summer so it should be fairly substantial. You have any number of options to choose from including trellis or tepees made from cane. Metal reinforcing grid of the type used when pouring concrete is another possibility. You will need to support it between two poles or lean two sheets against one another in a sort of A-frame, but if you do that the beans will quickly climb it. Though it may look a little more functional than aesthetically pleasing, the beans will soon disguise this.

I favour the tepee because they are easy to install. I simply force four canes into the ground at the corners of a square and then pull the tops together and tie them to make the tepee. I can grow beans up all four faces and, placed carefully they can add an architectural element to the garden, even if it is only a temporary one. You can provide cross stays by fastening shorter pieces of cane or just with string. Plant to the same depth as bush beans, and again, at about fifteen centimetres apart.

One attractive alternative to the tepee is to create a bean tunnel by making arches between two of your raised beds. Though not permanent, these arches need to be substantial enough to carry the weight of the plants and to stay in place for the whole season. Luckily you have the raised beds to use as supports so it is usually not too difficult to cobble something together. The beans will quickly grow over these to form plant tunnels. This utilizes space that you would not normally be used but it also makes for a very unique temporary feature. The beans will hang down into the tunnel and harvesting from underneath is very easy. At the same time, the tunnel provides a wonderfully shady place to sit with a garden magazine during the summer months and, in gardening terms, this officially counts as working.

Beans freeze very quickly so if you have an excess harvest they are a crop that you can continue to eat over winter. They can also be stored in sterilized mason jars.

CARROTS

Carrots are another vegetable that most of us consume on a regular basis. They are easy to grow and are well suited to the raised bed garden. In the ground, they are sometimes impeded by the presence of stones and rocks which tends to be less of an issue with raised beds. The soil the crop is being planted into has already been worked and allows for the unimpeded growth of these root vegetables. Carrots come in a far wider range of varieties than most people are aware of. There is a colour range which includes purple, yellow and black as well, as the more familiar orange, and they come in different sizes and shapes. Finger carrots can be eaten raw in salads while still very small, and there are round carrots and really deep rooted varieties. Overall, there are plenty of different options to consider and to experiment with.

Carrots don't like to be disturbed so you should sow them directly into your bed. You do this by sowing them into drills of one centimetre deep and fifteen centimetres apart. You will need to sprinkle the fine seed as evenly as possible which is sometimes a little tricky. To overcome this problem, mix the seed with some dry building sand and sprinkle by rubbing between forefinger and thumb. This makes the spread far easier to control.

Early varieties can be sown in the spring and you can cover them with some horticultural fleece if there is a risk of frost. They will need to be thinned to around seven centimetres as they develop. As they don't like having their roots disturbed you need to be gentle doing this or you can simply cut off unwanted plants with a pair of scissors. Maincrop Carrots are sown in late spring and they need only be thinned to every four centimetres. If you carefully pull up the thinnings you will have tiny miniature Carrots that make a sweet addition to salads. Keep sowing main crop carrots every two to three weeks up until midsummer for an ongoing succession.

Carrots should never be allowed to dry out as this encourages them to bolt. As long as the soil they are growing in remains slightly damp you can avoid this problem. Once harvested, carrots can be plunged into a bucket of damp building sand which can be stored in a cool dark place. This will ensure that you have a ready supply of fresh carrots for most of the winter months.

Just with these few crops, you will already be in a position to have a beautiful vegetable garden and dramatically reduce the amount of fresh produce that you need to purchase. You will also be introducing a far more comprehensive range of vitamins and nutrients to your diet.

Figure 26. Wonderfully imperfect organic vegetables.

EASY TO GROW VEGETABLES

There is a wide variety of other vegetables that are easy to grow and which at the moment you may not be eating regularly. Broad Beans are very easy to produce and are one of the earliest crops to harvest. That makes them an excellent vegetable to consider as the early rewards offer both motivation and encouragement. The same can be said for Radishes. They take up very little space in a garden and come through before just about everything else. They are so easy and quick that they provide a great motivator for small kids just being introduced to the 'grow your own' way of life.

Leafy greens such as Kale, Spinach and Chard are all high in vitamins and very visually pleasing. Peas grow easily and the Flat Snap Pea varieties are delicious when tossed in a hot frying pan for a few seconds or chopped and thrown into a salad. Garlic is easy to produce and in addition to being a useful plant to have in the kitchen, they also act as a deterrent to certain

Figure 27. Every time you eat is an opportunity to nourish your body.

pests while they are still in the garden. They make excellent companion plants to Carrots which can be attacked by Carrot fly. These pests detect the presence of Carrots by smell and the odour of growing garlic acts as a protection because it disguises their odour.

Cucumbers can be encouraged to climb up a trellis attached to one edge of your raised beds and they are another of those plants that we eat on an ongoing basis during the summer. In the next book on Advanced

Raised Bed Gardening we will look in greater depth at some of these plants as well as some more unusual plants like Pak Choi, Komatsuna and Sweet Potatoes. For the moment you have enough information to get growing and once you have got to grips with the various techniques in this book the next batch of information will not seem so overwhelming. Gardening is one of those subjects where one piece of information often becomes the building block for the next and in this, we are continually learning.

POTATOES

Before moving on, however, we need to look at one other vegetable that plays a massive role in the western diet. That is the Potato. Potatoes are eaten so widely that it would be remiss not to pay them some attention. The problem with Potatoes is that they take up quite a lot of space and if you have limited bed space you could find yourself in a position of having to choose between growing these or some of the other crops available.

Potatoes definitely will grow in a raised bed very easily if you do have space. Potatoes are grown from what are called Seed Potatoes which are just Potatoes that were bred to produce more potatoes. To grow them in your bed you don't even really need to dig them in very much. Simply place the Potato on the surface of the bed and then shuffle it around slightly until it is virtually beneath the surface. You can place the Potatoes every thirty to forty centimetres and they can then be covered with fifteen centimetres of compost or garden soil. The plants will grow up through the soil, pushing out side shoots as they do so. These shoots are where the Potatoes will eventually grow. When the leaves are protruding to around twenty or thirty centimetres add some more soil until just the top leaves are visible. This process is called earthing up. (Another professional sounding gardening term). The process can be repeated two or three times until the plant shows signs of flowering. At each stage, the side shoots will grow into the next layer of soil that you have added and the Potatoes grow on these shoots.

For the raised bed gardener, this offers several minor problems. The first is that Potatoes will take up plenty of your precious bed space. The second is that the earth you keep piling up tends to slide out of the beds and the third is that, come harvest time, the crop needs to be dug up.

Here is a far simpler solution that is space saving and easy. You need to get four old car tyres. Any tyre fitter will have heaps of these and they are more than happy to give them away. Place one tyre in your garden on a piece of weed proof membrane. It will need to be in full sun, but other than that can be put anywhere that is convenient enough for you to get water to occasionally. Next, you fill the tyre with the same soil and compost mix that you used to fill the top layer of your beds with. Tuck the growing medium into the tyre itself and gently firm down the mix. Once full, the tyre has effectively become a large pot. You now evenly space three of your chosen seed Potatoes. Cover lightly with soil and water them in.

When the plants reach twenty to thirty centimetres in height, add another tyre and gently fill it with soil and compost so that just the top few leaves are still showing. The plants will continue to grow and send out more side shoots. When they are high enough, you can add yet another tyre. When the flowers start to appear you will know that your Potatoes are ready, though it is a good idea to dig down a little and just check what they are looking like from time to time. If you are lucky you will be able to get to a depth of four tyres before you harvest, but even just three will provide a surprisingly bountiful crop. All you then need to do is pull the stack apart and gather the Potatoes. In effect, what you have done is create another raised bed using the tyres. This method gives you a very generous crop and at the same time leaves you plenty of space in your main beds. The system is easy to manage so you can grow as many Potato stacks as you think you will be able to eat. On average you should harvest three-quarters of a bag of potatoes per stack.

Figure 28. Even a small space can yield a respectable return on all sorts of potato varieties.

Potatoes can be stored in large paper or hessian sacks in any cool dark place and, providing they are not exposed to light, they will keep for months. Brush them down to remove any earth as it is dampness that will disrupt the storage process. Don't store them near your onions or any fruit you may be storing. These let off a gas which speeds the ageing process of the potato.

Some people feel that old tyres detract from the aesthetic appearance of the garden, but this is not necessarily true. As soon as the plants are in leaf, the appearance is perfectly acceptable and if you want to, you can go as far as painting the tyres in a colour that suits your garden design. They are also so easy to position that you can always tuck them behind a shed or elsewhere out of sight. If the tyres really offend your sense of the aesthetic then you can plant potatoes in a container such as an old barrel, bucket or even one of your Trugs. Whatever you opt for you will need to drill holes in the bottom. Though these containers are not usually as large as stacked tyres, they are portable and can be moved even when your potatoes are growing. There will be much more on container gardening in the fifth book in this series.

Figure 29. Colourful tyres to brighten up your garden design.

Now that you have a good range of vegetables growing, you might want to look at one or two other plants that will add value either to your diet or to the appearance of the garden. Herbs are always useful but are often overlooked. Many of the Mediterranean herbs such as lavender and rosemary are shrubs and though they can be incorporated into the garden design, they will be happier in the ground than in the raised beds. There are others, though, that will thrive in a raised bed environment.

The main requirements of most herbs are plenty of sun and a well drained fertile soil. The raised beds are therefore perfect. Many of the herbs will quite happily continue to thrive if you just clip off a few leaves when you need them. This allows you to have an ongoing supply of fresh herbs growing and still have plenty for your culinary use. When you see what the supermarket can charge for a few sprigs of thyme or a leaf or two of basil, then growing your own soon makes sense. If you have limited space such as a small raised bed on a balcony or patio, then herbs may be the best route both in terms of appearance and financial return.

If space is not too much of an issue, then it is worth thinking about dedicating one bed just to herbs rather than having them in several different places. As a general rule, most of the culinary herbs have similar growing requirements so having them together makes sense. Most of the herbs we eat tend to come from hot dry Mediterranean climates and it is easy to replicate this if you are doing so with just one bed containing plants with similar needs. Many are visually pleasing and produce flowers that attract beneficial insects.

Figure 30. Raised beds are perfect for your culinary herbs.

Often, people tend to ignore their raised beds during the winter months but this is really a bit of a mistake. Though there are fewer crops that can be grown over this period, it is the ideal time to work on the health of your soil and thus ensure that it is in the best possible condition right at the beginning of the following season. The soil will have broken down considerably by the end of autumn and it is now that you want to fill those beds up again so that there is time for the compost and manure to break down. All of those plants you have grown will have sucked up the nutrients and winter is the time to replace it. Fill the beds till they are overflowing as the planting mix will have sunk again by the time you are ready to start replanting in the spring. This is the time to throw in plenty of farmyard manure so that it breaks down and doesn't burn your plants.

There is another way to ensure that your beds have plenty of nutrients built into them by the next season. This involves growing what is called a cover crop or green fertilizer and, though often neglected by gardeners, it is really very easy and worthwhile to do this. Some crops actually bind nitrogen into the soil and this is the macronutrient that your garden plants are most hungry for. The idea is that you sow some of these crops in autumn and then just leave them over the winter months. Two weeks before you are ready to start planting the crops for the following year you cut them down and just dig them into the beds where they will break down naturally.

While the cover crop is growing, it binds nutrients into the soil and prevents both erosion and weed build up. As it breaks down it further improves both soil texture and nutrient levels so it is an easy win-win scenario. There are many different types of plant that fill this role but the best ones are members of the leguminous family as they have the best nitrogen binding ability. These include Crimson Clover, Alfalfa, and Peas though Fall Rye and Hairy Vetch also work well.

Don't worry if you still have an autumn crop in the ground such as late Chard. Just cast the seed of your cover crop and the chard will be ready to harvest long before the cover crop can swamp it. This is a technique known as underplanting which in widely practised in agriculture.

Some cover crops produce flowers which act as an early source of food for bees and other beneficial insects. Once the flowering period is over, however, cut the plants down before they go to seed or you could find yourself with cover crop popping up all over the show over the summer months, and in places you really don't want it. A simple whiz with a lawn strimmer will make this a straightforward task. Come the spring, the green fertilizer you have dug in will have rotted down and your nutrient levels will be perfect for the start of the new growing season. Of course, gardening does not need to be restricted to the warmer months and for those that can tolerate working outdoors during the colder weather, book ten in this series will be looking specifically at that subject.

START GROWING – RECAP:

- Decide on what crops you are most likely to eat. Use your shopping list as a guide
- Always keep a diary and records as this will prove invaluable in later years
- Choose between seed or seedlings. They both have advantages
- Growing tips for the more commonly eaten vegetables
- Consider at least some herbs
- Tyre potatoes offer space and labour saving possibilities

6

WATERING, FERTILIZERS AND PEST CONTROL

I n this chapter, we will be looking at three fundamental aspects of gardening that people often tend to overlook. Sowing and propagating tend to hog the limelight on the vegetable gardening stage. There is so much pleasure to be had from watching seeds emerge from their coatings and spreading those first delicate leaves, or the early green shoots forcing their way through the soil in a tyre planted with seed potatoes that the more routine stuff can seem a little lacklustre.

It is the routine chores that will make the difference between a successful crop and failure. All three of the subjects that we will be examining in this chapter play a crucial role in the garden. Their importance is augmented by the fact that you have chosen to garden in an environmentally responsible manner. When you choose to go organic you take a moral stand, and sometimes in life when we do that, we make things a little harder for ourselves. That is certainly the case when gardening without chemicals. You are no longer able to simply toss a handful of fertilizer over the bed and allow chemistry to supply the nutrients. Pest control ceases to be simply a matter of reaching for a spray bottle and annihilating an entire swathe of insects with just a few short squirts.

There are few areas in gardening that have been as contentiously debated as this one in recent years. There can be no doubt that when we decide to set aside the lethal insecticides and industrial fertilizers, we add an element of difficulty to our lives. I won't try to sugar coat that fact. More effort is required and yields will very often decrease, certainly in the short term. To counter that, however, the organic gardener can comfort himself with the knowledge that his crops do not contain toxic residues, he is not contaminating underground water supplies and he is not contributing to the massive decline in insect and wildlife populations that we have witnessed over the last few decades.

Figure 33. Insect hotel.

The benefits of the organic garden tend to be seen over a more extended period of time. The rewards are more nuanced and gentler than they are when you allow the big pharmaceutical companies to participate in your gardening endeavours. Gradually, over time, you will start to notice a change. That change will become more obvious as your eye becomes accustomed to seeing what benefits nature has to offer if we allow her the time to work her magic.

Figure 32. Ladybugs are beneficial bugs for your garden.

In the garden where pesticides are used, all insects become the enemy. There is no difference between a beneficial insect and one that will attack the crops, no innocent civilian or neutral bystander. The chemicals we apply do not discriminate. What is the point of being able to identify the aphid eating larvae of a lady-bird when it is going to be killed by the toxic mist that you blast the crops with. The organic gardener needs to become something of a cross between an entomologist and a soil scientist. Instead of just viewing his raised beds as a garden, the organic gardener needs to see the whole area as a small ecosystem.

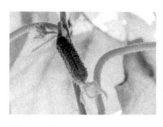

Figure 33. A baby cucumber can be found behind a female flower.

One in which he plays a large hand in managing. Over time, the organic garden evolves into a mini oasis, where insects thrive and the soil is rich. As if by miracle, birds will start to make an appearance and they will soon be followed by frogs, toads, newts and array of other creatures, many of whom will assist the gardener in the constant battle against snails, slugs and caterpillars.

Now that your beds are filled with soil that is rich in microorganisms and humus, and your crops are starting to make their first appearance, it is time to really ensure that your water usage is as efficient and well managed as possible. Unless you have a lawn of exotic grass blends, the vegetable garden is the area of the garden where most water is required and thus, where most water management needs to take place. Bear in mind that a single lettuce requires seventy litres of water to reach maturity. There's a shocking figure for you.

I mentioned earlier in this book that I would be revisiting the subject of mulch. This is an area that is very often ignored and one that I am passionate about. It is so easy to do, normally free and so good for the garden that I can never understand why people don't use mulch far more widely. It is crucial to retaining moisture, boosting soil condition and, of course, slowing down the rate of evaporation. At the same time, it smothers weeds and saves the gardener effort. On top of all that it is often free. What is there not to be passionate about?

Mulch can be any material that covers the soil surface and retains moisture. In decorative gardens, people often use visually pleasing mulches such as pebbles, broken slates or coloured wood chips. In the vegetable garden, I require more from a mulch than that it merely be pleasing to the eye. I want the mulch to be an organic material that will breakdown to add to my already healthy soil and there are many options to choose from. In keeping with true self sufficient tradition, I like the product I use to be homemade and cost nothing.

My preferred choice of mulch is always compost. As you first start gardening, you may only have a limited amount of your own compost available, but don't worry. This is one product that you will soon be producing plenty of. I like to lay it about six centimetres deep all across the surface of my beds, leaving small wells around the stem of each plant. Over time the compost will break down and become incorporated into the soil and our colleagues, the earthworms, love to drag it down and reduce my tilling at the end of the season. In the next book on advanced raised bed gardening, we will look more deeply at making compost, but although people have written realms on the subject, it really is very easy. Basically, compost is just broken down vegetable matter such as lawn clippings, leaves and all of those non-woody bits and pieces that the act of gardening, and cooking, produce on a constant and ongoing basis. This is then mixed with soil or manure and allowed to break down naturally to form a rich dark crumbly material.

Figure 34. Straw is one of the best mulch materials and provides your plants more of what they need to grow.

If you have any deciduous trees in your garden, then leaves will be one product that you acquire plenty of come the fall. Before becoming a gardener, you may have seen these fallen leaves as a nuisance. Now they become what organic gardeners refer to as black gold. Instead of burning them and pumping clouds of smoke into the environment, just heap them into a corner where they will break down into black crumbly leaf mould which is great to mulch with. Leaf mould is suitable for retaining moisture and adding texture but it does not have the nutrients that compost does. As the leaves break down, I mix them with farmyard manure and that breaks them down further and turns them into a sort of compost which in turn addresses the lack of nutrient problem.

Lawn clippings are very easy to get hold of even if you don't have a lawn of your own. I like to let them break down for a month before using them on beds that have vegetables growing in them, but they always make good mulch and soil conditioner after that. When you apply it you will be amazed at how much water they retain and how quickly they break down and get absorbed into the soil.

In your first season of gardening, you may not have easy access to any of the above mulches but there are still plenty of free options. Straw is cheap, light and makes an excellent mulch. At the end of the season, you can just dig it into the beds and let it break down naturally. Most tree surgeons and timber yards will let you have as many wood chips as you like and even shredded newspaper will do a good job of retaining moisture.

The mulch will act as a sort of blotting paper and prevent the top layer of soil from forming a crust off which water can simply run away. Once you have mulched your soil and are sure that texture is not an issue, then when you water is the next factor to take into account. A simple test of whether your beds are damp enough is to stick your finger into the soil. The top inch should be dry and after that, it should be damp but not waterlogged. It is better to water deeply and less often than to do lots of shallow watering. This encourages the root system of your plant to grow more deeply and thus it will be better equipped to overcome any dry spells. A deep rooted plant also accesses nutrients more effectively thus producing healthier and more tasty crops.

As a rule of thumb, the best time of day to water is the early morning or late afternoon. This cuts down on evaporation and allows the water to sink further into your soil. If your plants suddenly start to wilt then feel free to break this rule, but you will need to examine why they suddenly became water stressed. A healthy plant growing in a well conditioned soil should not need to be watered in the middle of the day and perhaps your mulch has become too thin or the previous watering was not deep enough. Don't water every day unless you have to. If the lower layer of soil is damp, then skip the watering until the following day. Weather conditions will obviously play a part in how much evaporation takes place. If it rains lightly, never assume that you don't need to water. Sometimes a drizzle is not enough to permeate the soil effectively. Just stick your finger into the ground an hour after the rain stops and see if it is still damp.

How you water is another factor to take into consideration. Simply turning on a sprinkler and allowing water to go everywhere is probably one of the least effective methods of applying water. It may be labour saving but this system is a far from an ideal solution. Not only will some of the water evaporate before hitting the ground, but it will also land in places where water is not required such as on paths. Wet leaves can add to the risk of moulds, blights and funguses and that can easily be avoided using less random watering techniques. Using a watering can with a fine rose on it eliminates the problem of poorly targeted water but ceases to be viable where you have several beds. In that case, a wand attached to a garden hose allows you to water at the base of your plants which is exactly where you want it.

If you buy a wand that only applies water when you pull a trigger that further increases effective water control.

Stepping up from the hose or can is the irrigation system. There was a time when irrigation systems were quite complicated and remained the domain of the irrigation expert. Today, systems are far easier to assemble and install and there is no need to pay for outside expertise. You can even buy battery operated timers that simply fit onto a standard garden tap and can be set to water the garden at a time, or times, of your choosing. The price is very reasonable and if you can set an alarm clock you can set a basic irrigation timer.

The irrigation comes in two basic forms. The first is a hose which you run through your beds and into which you plug either drippers or spray nozzles. I would suggest you avoid the spray system for the reasons we have just mentioned. The drippers work well but will need to be run to the base of each plant that needs to be watered. This can result in a complicated network of small pipes that are very easy to pierce during routine gardening options. I talk as someone who has some experience in this regard. The drip lines may seem neat and logical as you set them among your fledgling plants. As the garden develops and leaves start to flourish, all logic and preplanning seems to vanish and you have no idea where the drip lines go. That said, in plants that are less randomly placed such as tomatoes, there is still a place for drip feeders.

Figure 35. Drip irrigation system in a raised bed.

Another system is the leaky pipe system, and these too come in different versions. Both systems have a pipe that is run through the bed. One allows water to seep through it at any point as the pipe sweats. The other has a series of fine holes all along its length out of which the water can escape into the soil. In my experience, the sweat pipes have a shorter life span than those that are perforated. Both systems can be connected with simple joints and elbows to allow you to run the pipes up and down the length of the beds as you deem appropriate.

They can be pinned in place with simple wire staples that you can make yourself.

All of the above options require the gardener to do a few experiments. You will need to figure out how far from the pipe the water spreads and for how long the tap must run to supply sufficient water to all parts of the bed. Whatever kit you opt for, it will usually come with a set of instructions as to the width and depth of spread. I suggest you use this as a guideline but still do your own experiments. In general, a leaky pipe system will supply sufficient water to reach around thirty centimetres from each side of the pipe. For a four foot wide bed, you will need to run two lengths up each bed which is easy to do.

Irrigation systems, especially those that are timer controlled, can save the gardener a great deal of time and allow for holidays and away weekends. They are not fool proof, however, and all joints and connections need to be checked regularly. They are being put under fluctuating pressure from the water on an ongoing basis and if one of them pops open, you will end up with lots of water at the broken joint and none throughout the rest of the system. You can strengthen each joint by binding it closed with thin wire.

The other thing that all gardeners should consider is a water capture system. Even the small roof of a garden shed is enough to capture substantial amounts of water when fitted with gutters that lead to some sort of water butt. If all the rainwater that runs off an average house is captured then a gardener should never need to access mains water. Of course, even if you capture water, there is the question of how you then get it to where you want it. These days it is easy to purchase a small pump that will easily and efficiently transport your free water to your beds. Electric pumps come in two types. One is submersible and the whole pump is then dropped into the water reservoir and a hose leading from it carries water to the garden. The other has a hose that sucks the water from the butt to the pump and then it is pumped into the watering hose. Both options are easy to use and you will soon recuperate their cost in reduced water bills.

Things become a little more complicated if you do not have an electrical socket in a place that allows you to plug your pump into the electricity supply. All is not lost, however. It is easy to purchase a small pump that runs on either petrol or diesel fuel. These days, fuel pumps can be amazingly small and light and are easily lifted by even the least physical of gardeners. Before purchasing such an item, check with the supplier to ensure that the pump that you choose can push the water from your butts to your beds.

FERTILISING RAISED BEDS

Because you have opted to be an organic producer, you have taken away the option of just tossing a few handfuls of chemicals onto your beds to supply the nutritional needs of your vegetables. That certainly doesn't need to detract in any way from the quality of your produce and there are many ways of supplying your plants with food that don't involve the participation of large chemical companies. The first and most important issue is to ensure that your growing medium is of the highest possible quality. I have already mentioned this on several occasions and by now you will know how to do this. I apologize if I seem to bang on the drum of soil quality too often, but it really is the foundation of all good gardening.

Once your soil is in optimum condition, you will then need to keep it that way by adding nutritious natural mulches two or three times during the growing season. The plants will be grabbing nutrients as fast as they can and you will need to supplement what is in the soil to replace what the plants absorb. When you prepare the beds you can augment their nutrient levels by adding slow release natural fertilizers such as bone meal, hoof and horn meal or fish and blood meal. Because these are slow release fertilizers there is little that you can actually do wrong with them and they will not burn even the most tender of plants. You don't even need to dig them in if you don't want to. Before planting just sprinkle a handful per square yard and that fertilizer will slowly break down over the season. These products are very inexpensive but there is some cost and so here is a free alternative.

Plants like Stinging Nettles, Comfrey and Yarrow are known as dynamic accumulators. They have deep root systems and they suck up the nutrients from the soil in which they are grown. The nutrients then become trapped in the leaves. By making them into a liquid we get a homemade fertilizer known as fertilizer tea. This can be diluted with water and poured at the base of your plants every week or two. This ensures high nutrient levels no matter how much the growing vegetables absorb. These teas are perfect for heavy feeders such as Peppers, Cucumbers and Tomatoes.

*Figure 36. Comfrey leaves decompose into liquid rather quickly
and make a great liquid fertilizer.*

It is a good idea always to have a bunch of Comfrey growing in the corner of your garden. The plant is prized by herbalists who have been using it to heal wounds and broken bones for centuries. It is a hardy perennial and you can cut it back and harvest the large hairy leaves as often as four times a year. If the plant is established it will soon grow back with renewed vigour. The flowers are favoured by bees and other beneficial insects and, frozen into ice cubes, they add an interesting decorative element to summer drinks or sprinkled on salads.

Yarrow is equally undemanding and stinging nettles are one plant that you should have no trouble getting hold of. You will need a large dustbin or barrel with a fitted lid. Now you simply cut down the plant or plants, you are using and fill the bottom half of your container. Don't get hung up with quantities and percentages as so many articles and magazines suggest. Simply cram half the container with whatever of the three plants is easiest to come by, preferably a mixture of all three, and top up with water.

Some people like to weigh the leaves down with a brick or a rock but not only is this unnecessary, I advise against it for reasons that will become obvious. Now all you need to do is stir the mix every day or two. Gradually, as it matures, the water will turn dark and a noxious looking grey sludge will appear on the surface between stirrings. Don't be alarmed by this. It merely means that your magic potion is progressing well. A word of caution here - the mix smells really bad, especially if it contains a high proportion of nettles. Gardeners become somewhat accustomed to working with materials that may not be deemed sweet smelling by the less educated population. This one really is noteworthy, however. If you spill some on yourself it is capable of testing even the strongest of marriages, which is why I don't weigh mine down with a brick. I don't want to have to fish that brick out before I can use the mix and risk expensive divorce litigation in the process.

After three to five weeks, your mix is ready for use and you can carefully tip it into plastic containers such as large milk or fruit juice bottles. It will store in a dark room for up to a year. To apply it, you must first dilute it with water at a ratio of four to one and if you want to use it on smaller seedlings you should increase that ratio to eight to one. You can now water the base of each plant with the homemade fertilizer once a week and you are assured of a nutrient rich growing mix.

There will be a green to black mass of unidentifiable plant material left in the bottom of the barrel and this can now be poured onto the compost heap before starting the next mix. Over time you will reach a point where you just always have a barrel of this tea quietly brewing away in some shady corner of the garden. You will then have a constant supply of liquid fertilizer and there is no need to buy a chemical equivalent. You can feed your plants safe in the knowledge that you are not polluting the groundwater or poisoning the kids.

For an even more powerful concoction, fill a fabric bag such as a pillowcase with chicken manure and leave that hanging in a barrel of water for a month to six weeks. Chicken manure is really high in nitrogen which is the macronutrient that plants need most of. Used directly on the garden it can quickly burn plants, especially young and tender ones. If it is made into a manure tea like this, it can be diluted with water to a ratio of ten to one and you will have your own high nitrogen fertilizer that costs nothing. Once again, the smell is a little on the obnoxious side so handle with care and long rubber gloves.

PEST CONTROL

Ever since humankind started growing food we have had to compete with an array of pests. Some crops will be unaffected by one pest but will be vulnerable to another. Colorado Beetles, for example, love to eat Potatoes while Lettuce is the Caviar of the Slug and Snail community. Getting to know what pests to expect on what vegetables is a matter of experience, but all prevention is aided by close observation. Pests don't tend to just sit out in the open and make life easy for the gardener. They are sneaky little devils and they hide with as much cunning and expertise as the best trained guerrilla fighter. The first defence is always going to be a keen sense of observation. Look at the plant for signs of stress, nibbled leaves or hidden eggs. You will need to look under leaves and just below the soil surface carefully.

You also need to learn who your allies are. Ladybirds and their larvae are ferocious hunters of Aphids. The Blackbird and the Thrush both delight in Snails and

Slugs. Even the tiny Blue and Great Tits become carnivores during the nesting season. An adult bird will bring between 700 and 1000 Caterpillars to its chicks per day. That is a phenomenal amount and if that is what they need to feed their young, then you can only imagine how devastating the widespread use of pesticides must be to the bird population. As you abandon the use of pesticides in your garden you will witness an increased number of these allies taking up residence nearby. It is one of the most soul warming aspects of gardening. Gradually you reach a natural equilibrium in which the beneficial creatures keep down the pests to a degree where a healthy status quo is reached. That equilibrium is what the organic gardener hopes to achieve. Those that are not environmentally friendly must attempt to annihilate all competition using chemicals and, in so doing, destroy the beneficial creatures in the process. In effect, they must produce an arena that is perfect for their crops but a toxic desert for anything else. The organic gardener takes a far wider view.

Figure 37. Raised beds allow you more control over what's going on around your plants thanks to their design and construction.

Once you develop your eye and learn to spot insects, teach yourself to identify them. Ladybirds and Praying Mantises are a great asset in your garden and there are many others. You can either purchase a book on insects or a book on garden pests. Both will help you differentiate friend from foe. On the internet, you can purchase beneficial insects that will quickly colonize any healthy new environment into which they are released. Even large scale commercial growers are now starting to see the advantage of using bio bugs to attack pests. These come in the form of predatory wasps, mites and flies which thrive on pests that might attack your plants.

You can purchase them from breeders and then release them into your garden.

After observation skills, the next vital factor to consider is that insects will always attack weakened and diseased plants over healthy ones. Because you have prepared your soil and fed your plants so well, you have already put yourself at an advantage. Healthy plants are able to resist attack more efficiently and are better able to survive even when attacked. If you see plants that are looking weak or sickly, it might be a good idea to remove them rather than hoping they will limp back to good health. A fragile plant can act as a beachhead from which pests can launch attacks on neighbouring plants. Planting crops at the correct time also helps them to get established as they are not fighting their natural tendencies. They are quicker to get established and move beyond that vulnerable seedling stage more rapidly.

Another factor that works to the organic gardener's advantage is that we grow a wide variety of crops. Commercial growers tend to focus on just one or two crops and this, in turn, leads to the development of insect communities that thrive on that particular crop. By having a range of crops we prevent the build up of any one type of pest. Even when we do come under attack in one area, there are other plants that will remain pest free so that we still have a harvest.

Harvesting early is a defence mechanism that many gardeners overlook. Just as we like to eat our produce when it is perfectly ripe, the pests often have similar in tastes. Many fruit and vegetables will ripen perfectly well if picked just prior to ripening and then will continue to ripen when stored in an insect free environment.

Companion planting is another area that can bring huge benefits and we will be looking at this subject in some depth in book three of the series. Plants like onion, garlic, and even flowering plants like marigolds, have specific smells that either hide the presence of crops that pests favour or discourage the pest altogether.

There is no denying that when you choose to grow without the use of pesticides you are going to lose a certain amount of your produce to pests. That can be offset against the fact that in your raised bed you can grow a higher proportion of crops than you may normally have done elsewhere.

Despite all of the methods we have just looked at, there is no denying that suffering crop losses to thieving bugs and insects can be disheartening. Even the most organic gardener does not like to rely entirely on defensive methods. Sometimes you need to go on the offensive. Keen observation will help you spot your enemy and very often, in the case of Caterpillars and bugs, they can be removed and destroyed physically. Even the most faint hearted of gardeners can become quite aggressive if their vegetables are in danger. You will soon find yourself ruthlessly crushing beetles underfoot and picking off Caterpillars to feed to the Chickens in a sort of gladiatorial blood bath.

On the subject of chickens, these birds are voracious hunters of garden pests. When they are scratching away at the soil they are doing so to unearth creatures that would almost definitely be competitors for your vegetables. Chickens are a great asset towards pest control but only when you don't have a crop or they will quickly either want to share it with you or damage it with their digging. Letting them into the raised bed garden for a few hours each day while you prepare your beds is a good strategy but only if you are sure that you can keep them out later in the year. Ducks, on the other hand, are far less inclined to damage or eat your harvest but are experts at spotting snails and slugs.

Finally, there are non chemical pesticides. Many are available commercially but here are a couple that you can make yourself. My favourite is vegetable soap. This product can be sprayed onto any plants and will make them unpleasant to eat. When you have an invasion of Aphids, a spray bottle of this soap mixed with water will blast them away very effectively. Look out for Ants as these creatures farm the Aphids by moving them to the most tender shoots and leaves. The aphid produces a sticky liquid called honeydew and the Ants then eat this. If you spot Ants on the leaves of your plants then pay attention because it is almost certain that they are there in the company of their carefully managed Aphid flock. You can blast the aphids with the soapy mixture and they will get blasted off or simply slide away. Because the product is just soapy water you can augment this by rubbing the leaf between your fingers as you spray.

Unlike a chemical spray, there are no toxins that are going to kill other creatures or poison your produce. You need to be aware, however, that this is a short term solution and you will need to spray regularly or the pests will return. I carry a spray bottle with me and use it liberally against Aphids, Caterpillars and Shield bugs. You can get away with a strong concentration of dish-washing liquid and it will have a similar effect though, because it is thinner, it tends not to cling to the leaves as effectively.

To augment the power of your liquid soap you can boost it with crushed Garlic, Chillies or even a Nicotine solution made from soaking cigarettes in water for a few days. These all just add to the unsavoury effect that you are trying to create, though I find straight vegetable soap solution perfectly adequate.

When on the subject of building beds, I mentioned that it was possible to install physical barriers such as wire grills to stop moles and netting attached to the beds to discourage rabbits and deer. If you really have a significant invasion of insect pests, then there is no reason that you should not net off your beds with fine netting to prevent their access altogether. The raised beds facilitate this because it is so easy to attach either hoops or posts onto which the netting can be attached. Although it is comforting to have this option, I have never found it to be necessary because the raised beds provide such an ideal growing environment for my crops. They seem to quickly establish themselves and outgrow that stage where they are most vulnerable.

There will never be a time when the gardener can ever let his or her guard down entirely. Eventually, that all important observation skill simply becomes second nature and whenever you are watering, weeding or just wandering through the beds at the end of the day, you will find yourself turning leaves over and looking beneath the plants. As the environment starts to regain its natural equilibrium, you will begin to see a comforting amount of predatory insects and fewer pests. The bird population will increase and the soil will become a haven for worms. That is when you will know that you have really made a positive change to that tiny natural habitat that you have created.

Figure 38. Homegrown vegetables in raised beds patch.

PESTICIDES, FERTILIZERS AND WATERING – RECAP:

- A touch of the organic debate
- The magic of mulch
- Fertilizer teas
- The power of observation
- Predators and pest
- Good water management
- Irrigation options

7

COMMON MISTAKES AND
CHALLENGES

By now you will have gathered that I am a big fan of raised beds but it would be remiss of me to pretend that they are the fix all answer to gardening. In this chapter, I intend to go over some of the most common mistakes that new raised bed gardeners make as well as a few things that might make you want to consider other options such as planting directly into the ground. Most of the problems we will be looking at have relatively straightforward solutions, but at least you will have the whole picture and be able to make a realistic assessment of which route will work best for you.

First and foremost, there are the start-up costs. When you garden in open ground you prepare your soil and away you go. Raised beds require you to spend money before you can even get a crop into the ground. If you are lucky, you may be able to recycle materials, but the weight of soil puts pressure on the beds and those cobbled together with old doors and pallets are going to have a relatively short life span. As we don't like to use pressure treated wood because of the chemicals they contain, all wooden beds will eventually degrade. If you are using regular pine scaffold boards then you should not expect a life span of more than five years from each raised bed. Red cedar and some other types of wood will last longer, but even they are not a forever remedy. Some materials such as brick, stone and corrugated iron may indeed last for decades but the initial cost of their installation needs to be taken into account.

Figure 39. You will soon be ready to enjoy the nutritional benefits of homegrown leafy vegetables.

Raised beds require a lot of good quality soil to fill them in the first place and this can add to the initial outlay. This then needs to be mixed with garden compost and other more nutritious Ameliorants and, as you are just starting out, you probably have not built up your own supply and will need to buy some in.

Raised beds take time to build. They also need more forward planning than merely planting in the open. All of us, when starting a new project, are anxious to get going, but with raised beds, there is an awful lot of preparation work to do before we get to that delightful planting stage. If we don't plan the positioning properly or we put the beds together poorly, we will be punished at a later stage. Beds must be orientated correctly to take advantage of the movement of the sun and the preplanning is critical to ensure we have wide enough paths and access to things like water and compost.

If you are a fan of machinery such as rotavators, they can be more difficult to use in raised beds because you will need to lift the machine into the beds and then use it in a fairly confined space. Even when digging with just a fork or spade, you need to take care not to use the frame for leverage as this could cause damage. In my experience, there is less digging involved with raised beds and there is now a lot of research that suggests that excessive working of the soil can damage its microorganism population and its water carrying capacity.

Tall plants in high beds mean that some crops such as runner beans and taller varieties of tomato are that much higher than they would be if planted at ground level. For the shorter gardener, this could become an issue during harvest or when tying into frames and trellises.

Despite all of these issues, I still think that raised beds are something that most gardeners should consider. Now we will look at some of the most common mistakes that gardeners make when starting out with raised beds.

Many of the most common mistakes are made at the planning stage. Placing the beds too far from a water supply or orientating them incorrectly are the most frequently seen issues. If you design your beds too wide, then you will need to walk on them to get to the plants in the middle. This will quickly lead to soil compaction and eliminate one of the major advantages of the raised bed – accessibility. Keep beds to a maximum width of four feet unless you are seven feet tall or have arms the length of a Neanderthal. Next is making paths too small which is why I usually recommend keeping them as wide as a wheelbarrow with just a little bit extra so that the gardener can slide around the barrow without having to walk all the way around the bed. That said, there are plenty of instances where this rule would simply not be viable. With more and more people going down the urban farmer route, there is often a need to use as much growing space as possible. If this is your intention, then cut your paths to a width that you can walk down but be sure to consider that full grown plants will overlap the edge of their beds.

Raised beds can dry out faster than open beds, particularly if the soil does not contain enough humus. This will be most noticeable where the soil and the walls of the bed meet. If the soil becomes too dry it will contract and a gap will appear down which water will simply flow away. Two things will prevent this from becoming a problem. One is to ensure that the soil contains plenty of absorbent matter such as compost and the other is straight forward observation. If you are paying attention to your beds you will be able to resolve this long before it can become an issue.

A problem that is very rare with raised beds is that they become waterlogged. This will only occur if the underlying earth is very heavy with clay, or if there is a compacted layer beneath the original soil surface. Very occasionally this can occur if heavy machinery has passed over an area and compacted the subsoil to such a degree that drainage becomes impossible. If you encounter this problem, the short term solution is to dig small drainage trenches from the base of the frame. This will allow any water that is getting trapped to escape and you should be able to see out the season in this way. As soon as the season is over you will need to address the problem on a more permanent basis. Unfortunately, this will entail unpacking all of the growing medium from within the frame and then digging down until you break through the layer beneath that is causing the issue. After that the bed can be filled again. It is hard work but fortunately, it is also very uncommon. Usually when constructing the frames you pre dig the soil on which they will be positioned and this would alert you to any underlying issues.

Raised beds can be hotter in the summer months and colder in the winter. Obviously, a bed that is exposed to the sun on the sides and the surface will become warmer. In general, most vegetable crops will benefit from the extra heat. If you are planning on growing crops that have heat sensitive roots you may have to consider this but it is easily resolved with a little extra watering which will soon cool everything down. Another possibility is to install shade netting and this is something that gardeners in warmer regions such as South Africa and Australia are turning to more and more as the climate changes. The fact that you are using raised beds won't really make much difference and if anything, they offer an easy way to attach posts for supporting the shade netting itself.

In cooler regions where freezing takes place, then the cold comes into play. Generally, in these regions, the gardener is growing a hardy crop or a cover crop to turn into green manure the following spring. Here too, the temperature difference in a raised bed shouldn't affect your decision that much.

When planting crops there are other factors that the newer gardener sometimes forgets to take into account. Taller crops should be grown on the northern ends of the beds when growing in the northern hemisphere where the sun will be to the south. This stops them casting too much shade on smaller plants. The opposite applies in the southern hemisphere. The raised bed gardener will generally plant more densely than the open ground gardener. There are two reasons for this. The first is that raised beds often have a limited planting area and the gardener naturally wants to get as much of a harvest as he can from the limited space available. The second is that the more intensely managed growing medium simply allows the gardener to plant more crops and so therefore, why not?

When it comes to planting, one of the commonest errors, and this certainly is not restricted to new gardeners, is to forget to label the plant or seed that is going into the bed. It is easy to focus on the primary objective, which is planting and watering in, and then to forget what seems like a minor detail. If you have just spent an hour planting Tomato seedlings called Super Sweet it can't be that hard to remember, surely? The next day you plant Cherokee Purple and the day after that you pop in a couple called Early Girl. None of these are particularly difficult names to recall – at least in the short term. Come back a few weeks later, and unless you have been a particularly successful contender on the television show Mastermind, it is highly unlikely you will not know one plant from another. Add to that a few types of carrot, some bean varieties and some unidentified plants you scored from a neighbour, and your garden soon becomes a jigsaw puzzle which you will never be able to repeat, even if everything grows perfectly.

Record keeping is critical, and I dealt earlier with garden plans and the importance of a diary. It starts here with the planting. Every row of different plants needs to be labelled and dated. This allows you to see what plants perform best and to show off to any visitors as you casually throw out names and cultivars as you wander between the beds. Plant labels can be as simple as a lolly stick with the details written in indelible ink, or as ornate as individually cut pieces of slate or copper dangled from delicately twisted wire stands.

One other common error is to assume that once you have harvested all that is in the beds, all work is over until the following spring. If you just leave your soil bare over the winter months, many of the nutrients that the plants need will be leached out of it by the start of spring. It doesn't take long to cast some seed for a winter cover crop or to heap a rich mulch over the surface. When the spring comes, your associates the worms will have dragged much of the mulch deep into the soil. If the soil is left bare many of them will die along with billions of the other microorganisms that go into making a healthy soil.

The final, often repeated mistake is to not pay enough attention to your beds during the growing period. Even in inclement weather, you would do well to check on your plants every single day. They are living things, after all, and they depend on the gardener for their well being. This is important in both raised and open ground beds. By paying attention and re-staking early, a plant that has toppled over could well be a saved. Spotting a few caterpillars and crushing them along with any nearby eggs can make a huge difference over a twenty-four hour period. The time lapse between a few nibbled leaves and a seriously devoured plant can be remarkably short.

Figure 40. Homegrown crops in the evening light.

TACKLING MISTAKES AND CHALLENGES – RECAP:

- Failure to plan ahead can be disastrous
- Labelling and record keeping are critical
- The soil must be taken seriously
- You should use cover crops or mulch over winter

CONCLUSION

This book on raised bed gardening is the first of a series of books designed to lead the reader gently through the process of gardening in all its many different aspects. My objective in writing this series was to share the knowledge that I have gained over the years, but also to stimulate passion. Gardening is not merely a science or a collection of different techniques. It is also an art form, a therapy and a hobby that can become horribly addictive.

For some time I gardened using chemical pesticides and fertilizers. When I first became a gardener that was just what people did and anyone going down the organic route was considered a little bit of a fanatic. Over time I came to see that what the 'green fringe' was preaching was true. They were harvesting a yield that was comparable to mine but they could rest in the assurance that they were not harming the environment or themselves as they carried out their work. As I researched more widely, I reached a point where I could no longer keep pretending to myself that that was the case in my own garden. Scandal after scandal revealed instances in which the agrochemical industry either twisted the truth or abandoned it altogether to sell their chemicals.

It is hard to be a gardener without inadvertently becoming an environmentalist. Plants are a part of nature, after all, just as are we. To nurture a plant is to work hand in hand with nature. The more I delved into the world of chemical free gardening, the more it became obvious to me that it was not only a viable option, it was the only option if I was going to be true to myself. Although this series has followed an organic route, it is clearly not the only route and each gardener will have to decide for himself what principals to adhere to and which ones to set aside.

This book will have provided readers with enough information to get started as a raised bed gardeners. Although it only scratches the tip of the iceberg, for some it will contain all the information they ever need to fulfil all of their gardening ambitions. They will have learned how to make and position beds, how to fill them and how to maintain them. They also have enough information to produce some of the most commonly consumed vegetables, deal with the most frequently confronted challenges and care for the beds so that they are ready to produce another crop as soon as the next season allows them to.

We humans are not a species that is always easily satisfied. For many, the desire to take their gardening to the next level will become overwhelming, which is why I have written these books as a series rather than one large volume. If a reader manages to control the gardening addiction (highly unlikely), then this book will be all that they need. They will not have been forced to payout for information they will never use. On the other hand, if a gardener wants to build on the information in this book, they can simply opt for the more advanced follow up and they will have a whole battery of new plants and techniques to experiment with.

At whatever level a gardener decides to pursue this type of gardening, raised beds are just such a practical way to grow plants. The beds can be made at a size that will provide the vegetable needs for a whole family, or small enough to sit on the balcony of a tiny apartment. When placed on legs or built high enough, this method allows people who struggle to bend or who are partially immobilized, to continue to profit from the immense pleasure of growing plants for themselves. At both ends of that spectrum, the enjoyment and self-satisfaction can be immense. Whether it is growing large quantities of vegetables, or just a handful of herbs and ornamental plants, raised bed gardening offers the gardener a method that is both practical and attainable.

Figure 41. Organic urban garden in full growth at the end of summer.

Month	General	Tomatoes	Onions	Beans	Potato	Radishes	Carrots	Lettuce
Jan	Dig in cover crops or mulch heavily							
Feb								
March		Sow in pots indoors	Sow seeds or plant sets		2nd half plant seed potatoes		Sow first seed	Sow first seed
April		1st half harden off	Thin seedlings	Sow in pots	Earth up	Sow in drills	1st half sow 2nd half sow and thin	1st half sow + thin 2nd half Thin
May		2nd half plant out		1st half sow in pots 2nd half plant out	Earth up and liquid feed	1st half 2nd sowing	1st half sow 2nd half thin	1st half sow + thin 2nd half thin
June		Water and liquid feed		1st half plant out + stake 2nd half Harvest	1st half liquid feed 2nd half	1st half 2nd half harvest	Feed weekly	Sow
July		Water and liquid feed		Harvest	Harvest earlies Liquid feed and bone blood and fish meal	Harvest	Keep thinning where necessary Feed weekly	1st half 2nd half harvest
August		Water and liquid feed	Harvest and dry	Harvest	Liquid feed main crop	Sow again	Start harvesting Feed weekly	Harvest
Sept		Harvest	Harvest and dry	Harvest	Harvest main crop	Harvest	Continue to harvest Feed weekly	
Oct	Sow cover crops	Harvest	Harvest and dry Store excess		Store main crop		Continue to harvest Feed weekly	
Nov								
Dec								

ABOUT THE AUTHOR

Peter Shepperd is in his 40s and his interest in gardening started when he decided to give his family access to fresh, homegrown and organic food. Peter has been studying new gardening approaches to diversify his experience and skillset.

His experimentation has allowed him to figure out what works and what definitely doesn't. He disagrees with the use of pesticides and chemicals.

He has decided to produce this series of books to cover all aspects of growing, gardening and organic sustainability.

Peter has spent over a decade experimenting with different gardening techniques and perfecting his approach to growing fruits, vegetables, herbs and other plants. Not only this, but he has learnt how to make the most of each part of the food that he grows.

Teaching others has become his passion as some affordable, and straightforward practices have entirely transformed how his family gets access to healthy, delicious, nutritious and attainable food. Peter's vision is to slowly transition more and more people away from the often-tasteless vegetables that are purchased in supermarkets and are heavily reliant on the use of chemicals that are damaging the environment, towards homegrown organic healthy produce, believing that the process of doing so will also help grow the person that has produced them as well.

Peter lives with his family near Windsor in England.

THE BOOKS CURRENTLY IN THE GREEN FINGERED GARDENERS SERIES

REFERENCES

Figure 1. Elijas E. (2020). Yellow Banana Fruit Beside White and Orange Flowers. [photograph]. *Pexels.*

https://www.pexels.com/photo/yellow-banana-fruit-beside-white-and-orange-flowers-5503195/

Figure 2. Casap E. (2016). Bowl of tomatoes served in person hand. [photograph]. *Unsplash.*

https://unsplash.com/photos/qgHGDbbSNm8

Figure 3. Clarke S. (2021). Person holding brown and blask frog. [photograph]. *Unsplash.* https://unsplash.com/photos/q13Zq1Jufks

Figure 4. Spiske M. (2016). Carrots and onions in brown whicker basket. [photograph]. *Unsplash.*

https://unsplash.com/photos/ZKNsVqbRSPE

Figure 5. Sbytova M. Community kitchen garden. Raised garden beds with plants in vegetable community garden. Lessons of gardening for kids. [photograph]. *Shutterstock.*

https://www.shutterstock.com/image-photo/ community-kitchen-garden-raised-beds-plants- 1420905386

Figure 6. Footageclips. Raised bed with Lettuce Plants in the herb garden at the Convent Inzigkofen on Upper Danube Valley, Swabian Alb, Baden Wuerttemberg, Germany, Europe. [photograph]. Shutterstock.

https://www.shutterstock.com/image-photo/raised- bed-lettuce-plants-herb-garden-665071891

Figure 7. Zaitsev V. Strawberries bed covered with protective mesh from birds, protection of strawberry harvest in the garden. [photograph]. *Shutterstock.*

https://www.shutterstock.com/image-photo/ strawberries-bed-covered-protective-mesh-birds- 683104981

Figure 8. Urban F. (2021). Boy in black and white long sleeve shirt standing beside .gray metal watering can during daytime. [photograph]. *Unsplash.*

https://unsplash.com/photos/ffJ8Qa0VQU0

Figure 9. Viki2win. Mother and son working in a vegetable garden. [photograph]. *Shutterstock.*

https://www.shutterstock.com/image-photo/mother-son-working-vegetable-garden-1768998839

Figure 10. HOerwin56. (2016). Gardening tools old. [photograph]. *Pixabay.*

https://pixabay.com/photos/gardening-tools-old-used-worn-1478547/

Bayley L.H. [quote]. *Picturequotes.*

http://www.picturequotes.com/tools-of-many-kinds-and-well-chosen-are-one-of-the-joys-of-a-garden-quote-916826

Figure 11. Spiske M. (2018). Selective focus photo of shovel on sand. [photograph]. *Unsplash.*

https://unsplash.com/photos/pASHRAKiDeU

Figure 12. Kniez P. Green wheelbarrow in the garden. Garden wheelbarrow full of weeds and branches. [photograph]. *Shutterstock.*

https://www.shutterstock.com/image-photo/green-wheelbarrow-garden-full-weeds-branches-1686173887

Figure 13. Greenwood A. Wooden raised vegetable garden beds. [photograph]. *Shutterstock.*

https://www.shutterstock.com/image-photo/wooden-raised-vegetable-garden-beds-307824452

Figure 14. Congerdesign. (2016). Garden gardening hoe. [photograph]. Pixabay.

https://pixabay.com/photos/garden-gardening-hoe-garden-tools-1290801/

Figure 15. Prahl K. Closeup of a man using a pneumatic nail gun to finish the trim on cedar garden planters with sawdust flying. [photograph]. *Shuttertock.*

https://www.shutterstock.com/image-photo/closeup-man-using-pneumatic-nail-gun-1744796324

Figure 16. Vintagepix. Filling a newly constructed backyard garden box with soil. [photograph]. *Shutterstock.*

https://www.shutterstock.com/image-photo/filling-newly-constructed-backyard-garden-box-1374510545

Figure 17. Gunaydin N. (2014). Green metal garden shovel filled with brown soil. [photograph]. *Unsplash.*

https://unsplash.com/photos/BduDcrySLKM

Young P. W. [quote]. *Quotefancy.*

https://quotefancy.com/quote/1045307/William-P-Young-You-have-to-take-the-time-to-prepare-the-soil-if-you-want-to-embrace-the

Figure 18. Torneby E. (2020). Basket of mixed home-grown beans. [photograph]. *Unsplash.*

https://unsplash.com/photos/rNSg5Yo1k20

Figure 19. Kemper J. (2020). Person holding green plant stem. [photograph]. *Unsplash.*

https://unsplash.com/photos/4z3lnwEvZQw

Figure 20. Peredn) ankina. Spring green garden in a wooden box under the sun's rays. [photograph]. *Shutterstock.*

https://www.shutterstock.com/image-photo/spring-green-garden-wooden-box-under-647103319

Figure 21. Spiske M. (2020). Green plant on brown soil photo. [photograph]. *Unsplash.*

https://unsplash.com/photos/vCCeCZGcfSY

Figure 22. Spiske M. (2018). Fresh bio GMO-free tomtaoes - urban gardening self-support, self-supply with an old resistant breed. [photograph]. *Unsplash.*

https://unsplash.com/photos/I2qlS-51dgU

Figure 23. Spiske M. (2016). Onions in wicker basket. [photograph]. *Unsplash.*

https://unsplash.com/photos/mNA7PBweZy0

Figure 24. Estremera E. (2020). Green leaf plant in close up photography. [photopraph]. *Unsplash.*

https://unsplash.com/photos/clno5uJrr_k

Figure 25. Malréchauffé T. (2019). Green string beans on wooden bench. [photograph]. *Unsplash.*

https://unsplash.com/photos/YExVOSrJRNI

Figure 26. Stallcup B. (2018). Organic carrots. [photograph]. *Unsplash.*

https://unsplash.com/photos/b0IELTWBvT4

Figure 27. Skomal L. (2020). Brown and black handle knife beside green leaves. [photograph]. *Unsplash.*

https://unsplash.com/photos/ZZGo3YcGbaw

Figure 28. Waldrebell. (2016). Potatoes harvest. [photograph]. *Pixabay.*

https://pixabay.com/photos/potatoes-harvest-hands-earth-soil-5675693/

Figure 29. Sigmund. (2020). Yellow plastic round frame on green plant. [photograph]. *Unsplash.*

https://unsplash.com/photos/8k0G8yu1fVc

Figure 30. Wachowiak V. (2019). Green plant in pot. [photograph]. *Unsplash.*

https://unsplash.com/photos/k_88hrJYhrw

Figure 31. Meg G. (2019). Brown wooden house. [photograph]. *Unsplash.*

https://unsplash.com/photos/0Rzmbc-8i_4

Figure 32. Doukhan D. (2014). Raindrops leaf ladybug. [photograph]. *Unsplash.*

https://pixabay.com/photos/raindrops-leaf-ladybug-574971/

Figure 33. Alexei_other. (2019). Cucumber vegetables. [photograph]. *Pixabay.*

https://pixabay.com/photos/cucumbers-vegetables-food-healthy-4612955/

Figure 34. KaliAntye. Covering young capsicum plants with straw mulch to protect from drying out quickly ant to control weed in the garden. Using mulch for weed control, water retention, to keep roots warm in the winter. [photograph]. *Shutterstock.*

https://www.shutterstock.com/image-photo/covering-young-capsicum-plants-straw-mulch-1466467748

Figure 35. Alin_Kris. Drip irrigation. The photo shows the irrigation system in a raised bed. Blueberry bushes sprout from the litter against drip irrigation. [photograph]. *Shutterstock.*

https://www.shutterstock.com/image-photo/drip-irrigation-photo-shows-system-raised-1452131207

Figure 36. Moni08. (2015). Comfrey flower. [photograph]. *Pixabay.*

https://pixabay.com/photos/comfrey-flower-spring-violet-753174/

Figure 37. Du Preez P. (2020). Gardening. [photograph]. *Unsplash.*

https://unsplash.com/photos/JCZ2pE-Szpw

Figure 38. Maguire P. Homegrown vegetables in raised beds, vegetable patch in a garden, Uk. [photograph]. *Shutterstock.*

https://www.shutterstock.com/image-photo/homegrown-vegetables-raised-beds-vegetable-patch-1714017844

Figure 39. Hanna J. (2020). Green and red plant on white wooden fence. [photograph]. *Unsplash.*

https://unsplash.com/photos/hvSBya7hX2Q

Figure 40. Peredniankina. Spring green garden in a wooden box under the sun's rays. [photograph]. *Shutterstock.*

https://www.shutterstock.com/image-photo/spring-green-garden-wooden-box-under-647103334

Figure 41. Habich A. Organic urban garden in full growth at the end of the summer. [photograph]. *Shutterstock.*

https://www.shutterstock.com/image-photo/organic-urban-garden-full-growth-end-214541593